FLAVOURS SERIES

Delicious
Small Dishes

James MacDougall

Formac Publishing Company Limited
Halifax

Special thanks to **Craig Flinn**, chef and proprietor of Chives Canadian Bistro in Halifax, for preparing and styling the recipes photographed for this book.

Participating restaurants

British Columbia
Aerie Resort, Malahat, BC
Mahle House, Nanaimo, BC
Pacific Rim Grille, Coquitlam, BC
Raincity Grill, Vancouver, BC

Alberta
Teatro, Calgary, AB

Ontario
1505 North, Burlington, ON
Angeline's Inn and Spa, Bloomfield, ON
Black Cat Café, Ottawa, ON
Brookstreet, Ottawa, ON
Casa Bella, Gananoque, ON
Grosvenor's, Southampton, ON

Il Mulino, Toronto, ON
Little Britt Inn, Britt, ON
Signatures, Ottawa, ON

Nova Scotia
Charlotte Lane, Shelburne, NS
Chives Canadian Bistro, Halifax, NS
Fleur de Sel, Lunenburg, NS
La Perla, Dartmouth, NS
Onyx, Halifax, NS
Tempest, Wolfville, NS

Prince Edward Island
Dayboat, Oyster Bed, PE

Newfoundland
Aqua, St. John's, NL

Formac Publishing Company Limited recognizes the support of the Province of Nova Scotia through the Department of Tourism, Culture and Heritage. We acknowledge the financial support of the Government of Canada through the Book Publishing Industry Development Program (BPIDP) for our publishing activities.

Library and Archives Canada Cataloguing in Publication

MacDougall, James, 1966-
    Delicious small dishes : recipes from Canada's best chefs / James MacDougall.

(Flavours series)
Includes index.
ISBN 978-0-88780-730-5

    1. Appetizers. 2. Cookery. I. Title. II. Series.

TX740.M16 2007   641.8'12   C2007-903104-8

Formac Publishing Company Limited
5502 Atlantic Street
Halifax, Nova Scotia B3H 1G4
www.formac.ca

Printed and bound in Canada

Contents

Cuisse de Grenouille • Liquid Gorgonzola Grilled Cheese • Foie Gras Grilled on Rosemary Branches with Balsamic Syrup • Cortoni • Belgian Endive with Olive Oil-Tempranillo Dressing • Pheasant Breast Salad • Ancient Grain Salad with Soybean Tartar, Seaweed Salad and Wasabi Vinaigrette • Marinated Duck Salad • Mushroom Consommé • Black Truffle and Duck Consommé • Beet Soup • Green Olive Soup • Roasted Sweet Potato and Eggplant Soup • Roasted Parsnip Soup with Slow-Braised Crispy Pork Belly • Roasted Apple and Parsnip Soup • Carrot, Ginger and Lime Soup • Duck Shepherd's Pie • Prosciutto-Wrapped Quail Stuffed with Foie Gras, with Vin Santo Fig Jus and Braised Radicchio Treviso

Atlantic Crab Cake • Malpeque Bay Oyster Caesar Shooter • Seafood Tasting • Cured Peppered Halibut • Dungeness Crab Cakes • Corn and Crab Fritters • Poached Lobster Claw, Fiddlehead and White Truffle Flash, Chèvre and Apricot Twix • Pickerel Cheeks Poached in Tomato Consommé • Tom Yam Goong • Langoustines Simply Roasted with Espelette Chili, Tomatoes and Cured Fennel with Basil, Tomato Sabayon, Accompanied by a Small Salad • Grilled Spigola with Herbed Salad and White Balsamic Vinaigrette • Sauteed Finlayson Arm Spotted Prawn and Truffled Sooke Rabbit, Boudin Blanc with Black Truffle and Watercress Emulsion • Salmon Poached in Olive Oil with Arugula • Island Style Salmon Sashimi • Roast Celery Root Soup with Caramelized Digby Scallops • Diver Digby Scallops with Madras Curry Sauce • Seared Scallops with a Carrot Juice Reduction

Introduction

Small dishes are a relatively new concept in dining. The concept has evolved from the traditional Spanish tapas into a culinary trend now evident in many of the world's fine-dining hotspots. Small dishes give chefs the opportunity to introduce new ingredients and food combinations, to experiment and to show off their skills. And diners are the real winners — with smaller portions and more of them, many different flavours can be savoured in one sitting.

Chefs from across Canada have taken up small-dish dining with enthusiasm. Some of the country's finest chefs were invited to contribute to this book and their response was so overwhelming that it has been possible to present only a selection of the fabulous recipes they provided. However, the array of flavours that the chefs offered, reflecting Canada's varied regional cuisine, made preparing the book a joy. There is a wonderful mix of traditional, ethnic and regional flavours in these recipes. In many cases chefs have taken a traditional dish from their region or from their ancestry and infused it with new life by pairing it with something unexpected.

Many of these recipes reflect a strong sense of place. On the East Coast, dishes are drawn from the Annapolis Valley, where some of the finest fruits and vegetables in the world are grown. Root vegetables, tubers and fruit are all featured by our Nova Scotia contributors. The seafood from eastern Canada — as featured in this book's dishes from Newfoundland, PEI and Nova Scotia — is also amongst the best in the world. As we head west, we find chefs working with locally grown duck, pheasant, caribou and elk, along with locally grown fruits and vegetables. The Pacific Ocean boasts more great fish, as well as oysters, spotted prawns and crab.

We encourage you to follow the lead of the chefs when creating the fabulous dishes in this book: wherever possible take advantage of local produce offered at farmers' markets. You will be helping to support your local economy, reducing the environmental impact of the food you eat and producing dishes that are fresher and more flavoursome!

These recipes have all been tested and adjusted for the home cook — even the most gourmet-sounding recipes can be recreated in your own kitchen. Some of the ingredients in these recipes are relatively uncommon; when in doubt, ask at your local farmer's market, butchery or gourmet grocer. Read the recipes and plan your menus ahead, as some of the dishes require a little extra time. Once you have served them at a dinner party, however, your guests will assure you that your efforts have been worthwhile!

Belgian Endive, p.14

Appetizers — Land

The exciting variety of soups, salads and other small dishes featured in this chapter reflects the regional ingredients available to the chefs that provided the recipes. There are recipes for classic dishes such as the traditional French Cuisse de Grenouille from Lunenburg's Fleur de Sel. There are soups to suit everyone, from the rich and robust-flavoured Roasted Sweet Potato and Eggplant Soup from the Angeline Inn in Bloomfield, to the lighter, refined elegance of the Forest Mushroom Consommé from Grosvenor's in Southampton. For a different flavour, try one of the pheasant or duck salads or the unique Ancient Grain Salad from the Aerie Resort in Malahat.

Cuisse de Grenouille
(Frog Legs)

Fleur de Sel, Lunenburg, NS

An *amuse bouche* is a small starter used to stimulate the appetite. Here the frog legs are just the right size to start with. Lightly fried, crispy on the outside, tender and juicy on the inside.

1 egg
4 frog legs (pants)
½ cup (125 mL) flour
½ cup (125 mL) bread crumbs
3 tbsp (45 mL) olive oil
4 tbsp (60 mL) butter
2 cloves garlic, chopped
2 tbsp (30 mL) parsley, chopped
salt and pepper

In a small bowl beat egg. Dust frog legs in flour, dip in egg and coat with bread crumbs, set aside. In a large frying pan heat oil over medium-high heat, cook frog legs 1 ½ minutes on each side. Remove from the pan and place on paper towel. Drain oil from the pan and add butter, garlic and parsley. Melt over low heat.

Place a pair of legs on each plate and drizzle butter over.

Serves 4.

Liquid Gorgonzola
Grilled Cheese

Black Cat Café, Ottawa, ON

This is an adult version of a childhood favourite. The high fat content of the Gorgonzola melts so nicely in this taster. The powerful cheese surrenders its strong taste to the spiced pecans.

1 baguette
8 oz (250 g) Gorgonzola, sliced
2 tbsp (30 mL) soft butter

Spiced Pecans
1 tbsp (15 mL) butter
1 tbsp (15 mL) brown sugar
1 cup (250 mL) pecans, halves
1 tbsp (15 mL) heavy cream (35% m.f.)
juice of ½ a lime
½ tsp (2 mL) ground coriander
½ tsp (2 mL) chili flakes
pinch of salt
baby arugula leaves, for garnish

Preheat oven to 400° F (200°C). Slice 8 pieces of bread ½-in (1.5-cm) thick, on an angle to make long slices. Place 2 oz (60 g) of Gorgonzola between two slices of baguette, making four sandwiches. Press together well and brush both sides of each sandwich with lots of soft butter. Fry in a cast iron pan on both sides until golden brown. Transfer sandwiches to oven for 4 minutes.

To make the spiced pecans heat butter and sugar in a sauté pan until caramel aroma develops. Add pecans and sauté, being careful to avoid splatter. Coat nuts until very shiny. Add cream and lime juice and sauté until almost all liquid has evaporated. Add ground coriander, chili flakes and salt and transfer to a lightly greased baking sheet. Allow pecans to cool.

Serve sandwiches while still warm with spiced pecans and a few baby arugula leaves.

Serves 4.

Foie Gras Grilled on Rosemary Branches
with Balsamic Syrup

Casa Bella, Gananoque, ON

Foie gras is the fattened liver of, traditionally, goose, but nowadays usually of duck. It requires a delicate touch in cooking and is so rich that it is generally served with something sweet to balance the flavour.

1 cup (250 mL) balsamic vinegar
1 lb (500 g) foie gras
4 hardy rosemary sprigs
4 fresh figs
Maldon salt

Pour balsamic vinegar into a small, nonreactive pot and reduce over medium heat until the consistency of syrup.

Separate foie gras lobes and cut away any external veins. Cut foie gras (with a hot knife) into 4 oz (120 g) chunks.

Remove leaves from the bottom 2 in (5 cm) of rosemary stems, scrape ends clean and sharpen them to a point for easy skewering.

Cut figs in half and grill gently until heated. Set aside and keep warm. Skewer one piece of foie gras on each rosemary branch. Salt and grill using a foil shield to prevent rosemary from burning. Cook 45 seconds on each side.

Arrange figs and foie gras skewers on 4 plates and serve immediately, drizzling balsamic syrup around plate and seasoning with Maldon salt.

Serves 4.

Cortoni

La Perla, Dartmouth, NS

Cortoni is the name given to side dishes in Italy. Generally, main meals are served without any vegetable or starch — these are served as a course of their own. Here I have chosen vegetables that go well with saltimbocca. See page 94.

4 baby artichokes
8 baby potatoes
1 bunch rappini
¼ cup (65 mL) extra virgin olive oil
8 slices pancetta, diced
12 grape tomatoes
salt and pepper
2 tbsp (30 mL) balsamic vinegar

Place a large pot of water on high heat to boil, and add a good amount of salt. Prepare artichokes by removing the ends, peeling off the tough outer leaves and peeling the stem. Cut artichokes in half and cook in salted water until tender. Remove and keep warm. Cook potatoes in the same water until tender and keep warm. Blanch rappini in fresh boiling water and drain. In the same cooking pot add olive oil and sauté vegetables, pancetta and tomatoes until flavours mix and all is warm. Season with salt and pepper and add vinegar.

Divide vegetables equally between four plates.

Serves 4.

Belgian Endive
with Olive Oil-Tempranillo Dressing

Black Cat Café, Ottawa, ON

Belgian endive is a member of the chicory family, so it is slightly bitter. The fragrant wine combined with the flowery honey and vanilla bean make this starter salad a must, accompanied by the same wine for drinking.

1 cup (250 mL) Tempranillo red wine
1 tsp (5 mL) ground coriander seed
2 tbsp (60 mL) honey
1 vanilla bean, scraped
3 tbsp (45 mL) sherry vinegar
½ tsp (2 mL) sea salt
¾ cup (190 mL) pure olive oil
4 Belgian endives
4 oz (120 g) shaved Manchego cheese

In a small saucepan simmer red wine, coriander, honey and vanilla until reduced by two-thirds. Remove from heat and cool, add sherry vinegar and salt and whisk in olive oil in a thin stream until emulsified. Transfer to a squeeze bottle and refrigerate up to 3 days.

Cut endives in half lengthwise, rub with olive oil and grill, cut-side down about 4 minutes.

Divide grilled endives between 4 plates, drizzle with red-wine vinaigrette and surround with shaved Manchego cheese.

Serves 4.

Pheasant Breast
Salad

Angeline's Inn and Spa, Bloomfield, ON

Pheasant is a game bird that seems to hold a mystery. Just remember it's similar to chicken, but with ten times the flavour. Duck always makes a great alternative to pheasant.

1 pheasant breast 6 oz (180 g)
1 tsp (5 mL) shallots
1 tbsp (15 mL) white wine
1 tbsp (15 mL) balsamic vinegar
1 tsp (5 mL) butter
mixed salad greens

Salad Vinaigrette
2 tbsp (30 mL) olive oil
1 tbsp (15 mL) balsamic vinegar
1 tbsp (15 mL) pumpkin seed oil
salt and pepper
½ Granny Smith apple, julienned

Yields ¼ cup (60 mL)

Preheat oven to 300°F (150°C). In a small sauté pan sear pheasant breast on both sides over medium-high heat, then roast slowly in oven until desired doneness. Remove from oven and let rest on a plate tented with foil wrap to keep warm.

Discard fat from sauté pan, add chopped shallots and cook until light in colour. Deglaze pan with white wine, add balsamic vinegar and butter to make a vinaigrette for the pheasant.

Toss salad greens with olive oil, vinegar, pumpkin seed oil, salt and pepper.

Divide salad between plates, slice pheasant breast, dress over salad and sprinkle balsamic vinaigrette over meat. Sprinkle salad with julienne of apple.

Serves 4.

Ancient Grain Salad with Soybean Tartar,
Seaweed Salad and Wasabi Vinaigrette

Aerie Resort, Malahat, BC

Old is always new and the ingredients in this salad seem to say it all.

Ancient Grain Salad

2 oz (60 g) kamut kernels
2 oz (60 g) spelt kernels
1 oz (30 g) quinoa kernels
1 medium shallot
1 clove garlic
1 oz (30 g) edamame (fresh soy beans)
salt and pepper

Seaweed Salad

1 oz (30 g) mixed sprouts
3 oz (90 g) fresh herbs (chives, chervil, parsley, etc.)
2 oz (60 g) fresh seaweed (dried dashi kombu,
   dulse or similar can be substituted)
4 tsp (20 mL) lemon oil

Wasabi Vinaigrette

½ oz (15 g) wasabi
juice of 1 lemon
1 oz (30 mL) rice vinegar
½ oz (15 mL) honey
3 oz (90 mL) grapeseed oil
1 oz (30 g) fresh soybeans

Soak kernels in cool water 12 to 24 hrs. Blanch soybeans and peel outer layer. Reserve.

For the salad, mix sprouts with fresh herbs. Wash seaweed, dry and chop to a fine julienne. Add to herb and sprout mix and set aside.

Make wasabi vinaigrette by placing all ingredients in a blender and blending on high speed 1 minute. Adjust seasoning and strain through fine mesh sieve. Reserve.

Boil three types of kernels separately in salted water until tender. Rinse under cold water and drain. Add chopped shallot, garlic and soybeans. Add enough of wasabi vinaigrette to bind grains together. Season to taste.

Place 2 tablespoons of wasabi vinaigrette in the centre of the plate. In the vinaigrette place a 3-in (7.5-cm) ring and pack in 5 tablespoons of grain mixture, then remove ring. Season seaweed salad with lemon oil and place on top of grain tartar. Serve chilled.

Serves 4.

Marinated Duck
Salad

Mahle House, Nanaimo, BC

The rich smoky duck is a perfect match for the earthiness of the shiitake mushroom vinaigrette.

2 tbsp (30 mL) canola oil
2 smoked duck breasts

Shiitake Vinaigrette
¼ cup (65 mL) tomato juice
¼ cup (65 mL) rice vinegar
¼ cup (65 mL) soy sauce
¼ cup (65 mL) olive oil
1 tbsp (15 mL) sugar
1 cup (250 mL) sautéed shiitake mushrooms
8 oz (250 g) mixed greens

Preheat oven to 500°F (260°C). Heat a sauté pan with a little oil to high temperature. Add duck breasts, skin side down, and brown. Transfer to oven, skin side up, and bake 5 minutes. Remove and let rest 5 minutes.

Place all shiitake vinaigrette ingredients in a bowl and whisk to combine.

Julienne the duck and toss with greens and vinaigrette. Divide between 4 plates.

Serves 4.

Mushroom
Consommé

Grosvenor's, Southampton, ON

The taste of this soup really depends on the mushrooms you use. Try to get as many different varieties as possible. Dried porcini (also known as cepes) will lift the flavour dramatically.

3 lb (1.5 kg) mixed mushrooms
1 large carrot, diced
3 small onions, diced
3 ribs celery, diced
½ fennel bulb, diced, fronds reserved
2 garlic bulbs, cut in half
2 tbsp olive oil
1 cup (250 ml) white wine
12 cups (3 L) chicken stock

Clarification Raft
1 chicken breast, raw
½ small carrot
1 celery rib
1 ½ cups (375 mL) egg whites

Fennel Oil Garnish
reserved fennel fronds
1 cup canola oil
julienned cepes and enoki mushrooms,
    for garnish

On a baking sheet place mushrooms and toast in a 300°F (150°C) oven 15 minutes. In a large pan sauté carrot, onions, celery, fennel and garlic in olive oil until browned and nicely caramelized. Deglaze pan with wine, pour vegetables into a large pot and add mushrooms. Add chicken stock and simmer 2 hours. Cool and refrigerate overnight. Pour soup through a fine sieve lined with cheesecloth. Pour into a clean pot and begin to clarify.

In a food processor place chicken breast, carrot and celery and purée until quite fine. Beat egg whites until stiff peaks appear and blend with vegetable purée. Place this mixture into the pot of cold mushroom stock and heat on medium-low heat. The mixture will begin to slowly float to the top forming a raft, gathering impurities as it rises. Remove raft after about 20 minutes and discard. Strain consommé through a fine sieve lined with cheesecloth.

For the fennel oil, blanch reserved fennel fronds in a pot of boiling water 30 seconds, then shock in ice water. Squeeze as much water as possible from fronds, place in a blender with canola oil and purée until green and smooth. Set aside.

Divide consommé between bowls, garnish with julienned cepes, enoki mushrooms and a few drops of fennel oil.

Serves 6.

Black Truffle
and Duck Consommé

Teatro, Calgary, AB

A consommé should be as clear as you can make it. It is generally light flavoured, and the garnish should sing its praises in perfect harmony.

6 cups (2.5 L) duck stock (recipe follows)
¼ large onion, finely diced
¼ large carrot, finely diced
¼ celery stalk, finely diced
1 sprig fresh thyme
¾ tbsp (12 mL) whole white peppercorns
¼ fresh bay leaf
½ tomato, diced in large pieces
3 egg whites, lightly beaten

Garnish
1 carrot
1 parsnip
1 rib celery
1 black truffle

Place duck stock in a tall pot. In a separate bowl mix together all other ingredients except the garnish. Place mixture into stock while stock is still cold. Heat slowly, without letting liquid come to a boil. Stir once or twice so the mix doesn't stick to the pot. The stock should come to a light simmer, when the mixture will float to the top. Once this happens, stop stirring. This is called a raft; the coagulation of the eggs is what clarifies the stock. Let stock simmer 30 minutes, then turn off the heat and let consommé cool on the stove. When cool, the raft will fall. Ladle out consommé without disturbing the raft or you may cause cloudiness, which would defeat the purpose of clarifying.

Finely dice carrot, parsnip and celery. Shave four slices of black truffle and finely dice. Place finely diced garnish in a serving bowl and ladle soup into the bowl. Truffle oil can be used in place of fresh truffles but adds a little oiliness to the soup.

Duck Stock
bones from 2 ducks
1 carrot
1 medium onion
2 ribs celery
1 tbsp (15mL) black peppercorns
1 oz (30 g) parsley
2 tbsp (30 ml) tomato paste

Place duck bones and vegetables in a large roasting pan and cook in an oven at 350ºF (180ºC) until bones begin to brown. Remove from the oven and spread tomato paste over bones; continue to roast until dark brown but not burnt. Place all ingredients in a stock pot, add enough water to cover and bring to a boil. Reduce heat and simmer 1 ½ hours. Strain, reserving liquid and discarding bones and vegetables.

Serves 8.

Beet Soup

Pacific Rim Grille, Coquitlam, BC

Fennel adds a new taste to borscht. The soft liquorice aroma shines through in the flavour of this soup.

2 lb (1 kg) beets, blanched
½ cup (125 mL) canola oil
1 fennel bulb, diced
1 medium onion, diced
2 star anise
1 cup (250 mL) red wine vinegar
1 ½ cup (375 mL) sugar
8 cups (2 L) chicken stock
1 bay leaf
1 tsp (5 mL) salt
1 tsp (5 mL) pepper
2 cups (500 mL) yogurt

Peel and chop beets. In a large pot heat oil over high heat and sweat onion. Add remaining ingredients except yogurt, and simmer until beets are cooked. Add yogurt, bring back to a boil and cool. Serve.

Serves 4.

Green Olive
Soup

Fleur de Sel, Lunenburg, NS

A classic soup, some say the original of the famous Spanish gazpacho. This type of soup is found in many Mediterranean countries where olives are grown.

2 ½ oz (75 g) diced leek (green part only)
1 ½ oz (50 g) green pepper, diced
5 oz (175 g) celery
5 oz (175 g) onion, diced
1 ¾ lb (850 g) green olives, sliced
1 oz (35 g) garlic
⅔ oz (20 g) cumin
2 tbsp (30 mL) olive oil
6 cups (1 ½ L) water
green food colouring
croutons, chopped tomato, basil, chopped black
 olive and grilled shrimp, as optional garnish

In a large pot, sauté leeks, green pepper, celery, onion, olives, garlic and cumin in olive oil until soft. Pour in enough water to just cover and bring to a boil. Pour into a blender and purée until smooth. Add a little green food colouring to enhance, refrigerate until completely chilled, garnish with croutons, chopped tomato, basil, chopped black olive and grilled shrimp if desired.

Serves 4.

Roasted Sweet Potato
and Eggplant Soup

Angeline's Inn and Spa, Bloomfield, ON

Roasting the eggplant brings a whole new dimension to the fruit. It becomes very soft and the sweetness comes alive. Blended with the caramelized natural sugars in the sweet potato they create this amazing soup.

1 medium sweet potato
1 medium eggplant
1 Spanish onion
3 tbsp (45 mL) olive oil
1 tsp (5 mL) butter
2 garlic cloves, whole
2 cups (500 mL) chicken stock
¼ cup (65 mL) heavy cream (35% m.f.)
salt and pepper
fresh chive

Poke sweet potato and eggplant with fork, place on a baking tray, sprinkle with olive oil and roast at 400°F (200°C) until soft (eggplant will take less time than potato).

Remove skins of eggplant and potato and discard. While sweet potato and eggplant are roasting, dice onion and sweat in a medium-sized pot with olive oil and butter until golden brown. Add garlic, sweet potato and eggplant, pour in chicken stock and simmer 15 minutes to extract flavours. Purée smooth with a hand blender, add cream, check seasoning and adjust.

Serve and garnish soup with finely cut fresh chive.

Serves 4.

Roasted Parsnip Soup
with Slow-Braised Crispy Pork Belly

Onyx, Halifax, NS

Pork belly is gaining new ground in the restaurant industry. This is the same cut used in making bacon strips. The ratio of meat to fat is small, but the taste is huge. The fat in the belly melts through the meat and melts in your mouth. Brining the meat opens it to allow more flavour in.

½ cup (125 mL) chicken stock
1 ¼ cups (312 mL) milk (3.25% m.f.)
2 tbsp (30 mL) onions, chopped
1 garlic clove, peeled and chopped
2 tbsp (30 mL) olive oil
6 ½ oz (200 g) parsnip, peeled and chopped
1 tsp (5 mL) salt
2 tsp (10 mL) butter, unsalted
2 thyme sprigs
1 small bay leaf
4 parsley stalks
¼ celery rib
2 tsp (10 mL) white wine, boiled

Brined Pork Belly
12 cups (3 L) water
10 oz (300 g) table salt
½ lemongrass stalk
½ garlic bulb
1 rosemary sprig
1 cinnamon stick
3 sprigs thyme
4 ½ bay leaves
4 star anise
3 oz (90 g) coriander seed
1 oz (30 g) ginger
1 lb (500 g) pork belly

Bring chicken stock and milk to a boil. In a large pan sweat onions and garlic with butter and oil, add parsnips and cook until soft and lightly coloured. Pour in chicken stock mixture, herbs, celery and wine and simmer until parsnips are soft. Purée in a blender until smooth, adjust seasoning and pass through a fine sieve. Set aside.

Mix all brining ingredients in a pot and bring to a boil. Remove from heat and cool completely. Cover pork belly with brine and refrigerate 24 hours. Remove from brine and rinse off. In a roasting pan, cover pork belly with cool water. Cover with tin foil and place in a 200°F (100°C) oven 12 hours. Once cooked, drain and press out as much liquid as possible and refrigerate overnight. Next day cut pork belly into small cubes and fry until golden brown and crispy. Store in an airtight container until required.

To assemble, place three cubes of pork belly in a soup bowl and pour warm soup around.

Serves 4.

Roasted Apple
and Parsnip Soup

Tempest, Wolfville, NS

The Annapolis Valley, where Tempest is located, is famous for its apples and produce. The sweetness of the apples and the slightly bittersweet taste of parsnips scream with flavour when their natural sugars are caramelized.

1 lb (450 g) parsnips, peeled
1 celeriac, peeled and chopped into large pieces
2 lb (1 kg) Gala apples, quartered and seeded
3 tbsp (45 mL) olive oil
10 sprigs fresh thyme
salt and pepper
2 tbsp (30 mL) butter
1 carrot, peeled and diced
1 onion, peeled and diced
2 ribs celery, diced
1 small fennel bulb, diced
1 tsp (5 mL) chopped garlic
½ tsp (3 mL) chopped ginger
¼ tsp (2 mL) nutmeg
3 cups (750 mL) vegetable stock
3 cups (750 mL) apple cider
salt and pepper
¼ cup (65 mL) heavy cream (35% m.f.), optional

Preheat oven to 400°F (200°C). Rub parsnips, celeriac and apples with 2 tbsp (30 L) olive oil and toss with thyme, salt and pepper. Place in a roasting pan and roast in the oven 12 to 15 minutes or until a little brown colouring appears on apples and parsnips. Remove from the oven and cool.

In a soup pot over medium heat, melt butter and remaining oil. Add carrot, onion, celery and fennel and sauté 10 minutes or until onions are translucent. Add parsnip and apple mixture, garlic, ginger and nutmeg and sauté another 5 minutes. Do not allow garlic or ginger to burn. Add stock or water and cider to cover vegetables and bring to a boil. Simmer 30 to 40 minutes, adding more water if level goes down.

Remove from stove, cool and purée in a blender, strain through a fine mesh strainer, return to the pot and reheat to a simmer. Adjust seasoning with salt and pepper, and add cream and a nub of butter, if desired.

Serves 6.

Carrot, Ginger and Lime
Soup

1505 North, Burlington, ON

The lime juice awakens the ginger and gives new life to a classic soup that is always great. It will certainly spark the attention of your dinner guests.

1 ¼ lb (625 g) carrots, peeled
4 cups (1 L) chicken stock
2 in (5 cm) ginger, grated
juice and zest of 4 limes

In a large pot cook carrots in stock until soft. In a food processor, purée carrots with enough stock to form a medium-consistency soup, add ginger and lime juice and process again. Return soup to the pot and heat through. Garnish with lime zest.

Serves 4.

Duck Shepherd's Pie

Brookstreet, Ottawa, ON

The legs of the duck hold bold flavour, but require tenderizing. Braising is the way to go. Long slow cooking will help break down the meat to make it fork tender.

4 duck legs
3 cups (750 mL) Cabernet Sauvignon
2 carrots, ¾-in (2-cm) dice
2 celery, ¾-in (2-cm) dice
1 medium onion, ¾-in (2-cm) dice
3 thyme sprigs
1 bay leaf
1 bulb of garlic
salt and pepper
5 tbsp (75 mL) vegetable oil
5 tbsp (75 mL) tomato paste
4 oz (120 g) all-purpose flour
4 cups (1 L) chicken or veal stock
5 medium Yukon gold potatoes, peeled
1 celery root, peeled
¾ cup (190 mL) heavy cream (35% m.f.)
2 ½ oz (80 g) Parmesan cheese
2 ½ tbsp (45 g) sweet butter
4 oz (120 g) apple wood cheddar cheese

In a large bowl combine duck legs, warmed wine, carrots, celery, onion, thyme, bay leaf and halved head of garlic. Marinate in the refrigerator overnight. The following day, remove legs and vegetables, keeping them separate. Reserve marinade.

Pat duck legs dry and season with salt and pepper. In a large roasting pan sear duck legs until golden brown, starting skin side down. Drain excess fat, wipe the roasting pan clean and add vegetable oil over medium heat.

Sauté reserved carrot, celery and onions until golden brown. Stir in tomato paste until it melts, then stir in flour. Turn heat to high and add reserved marinade liquid. Bring to a boil and reduce by half.

Return browned legs to the pot and add stock. Return to a boil again and cover the pot with a tight-fitting lid.

Cook in a 375°F (190°C) oven 3 to 4 hours until meat is very tender and falling off the bone.

Continued on p. 30.

Duck Shepherd's Pie
(Continued)

While duck legs are cooking prepare vegetables. Cut potatoes and celery root into medium dice. In a large pot cover vegetables with cold salted water and cook 25 minutes. Strain and pass vegetables through a food mill, stir in cream, Parmesan and butter and adjust seasoning. Set aside and keep warm.

Remove duck legs from stock, strain cooking liquid and transfer to a saucepan. Reserve solids, but remove bay leaf, thyme leaf and garlic remnants. Skim duck fat from sauce using a ladle. Set sauce over a high flame and reduce by one-half, skimming as required. There should be about 1 ½ cups (375 mL) of sauce left over.

When duck legs are cool enough to touch, remove fatty skin and pull meat from bones. Discard all fat and bones. Combine duck meat with reserved cooked vegetables from marinade.

Pour in just enough sauce to loosely bind duck and vegetables.

Place a 6-in (15-cm) round form on the plate and pack duck confit into the form, using the base of a bottle smaller than the form. Spoon a layer of mashed potato on top and level. Remove the form. Sprinkle the plate with grated apple wood cheddar cheese and torch the plate with a blowtorch. Spoon reserved sauce from duck onto the plate. Serve immediately.

Serves 4.

Prosciutto-Wrapped Quail Stuffed with Foie Gras,
with Vin Santo Fig Jus and Braised Radicchio Treviso

Il Mulino, Toronto, ON

Classic Italian, these little game birds are just the right size. The saltiness of the prosciutto works well with the sweet Vin Santo and well-aged balsamic vinegar.

4 boneless quail
½ tsp (2 mL) chopped rosemary
½ tsp (2 mL) chopped thyme
4 ½ oz (135 g) salt-cured foie gras
4 slices prosciutto
1 cup (250 mL) Vin Santo
1 tbsp (15 mL) honey
8 mission figs
2 tbsp (30 mL) aged balsamic vinegar of
   Modena
2 heads radicchio Treviso
1 tbsp (15 mL) butter
1 tbsp (15 mL) extra virgin olive oil
1 cup (250 mL) chicken stock
salt and pepper

Stuff quail with rosemary, thyme and foie gras. Wrap with prosciutto and set aside.

In a pot, pour in wine and honey and add figs. Cook over medium-low heat and reduce to a syrup. Add vinegar. Cut radicchio in quarters, then pan sear with butter and olive oil. When slightly caramelized, add chicken stock, salt and pepper, then braise in oven at 350°F (180°C) approximately 10 minutes.

Roast quails 8 to 10 minutes at 450°F (230°C), or until golden brown in colour.

Place 2 pieces of radicchio on each plate, followed by 1 quail and 2 figs. Spoon syrup around quail and radicchio.

Serves 4.

Poached Lobster Claw, Fiddlehead and White Truffle Flash, Chèvre and Apricot Twix, p. 42.

Appetizers — Sea

The waters within and surrounding Canada offer a bounty of delicious edible creatures, and many of them are showcased in this stunning array of dishes. The Seafood Tasting from Aqua in St. John's features three types of fish and their innovative accompaniments — a great way to start a dinner party. If you are in the middle of the country there are great freshwater fish like pickerel, as featured in the Little Britt Inn's Pickerel Cheeks Poached in Tomato Consommé — and what a fight it can put up if you have time to do a little fishing! The Poached Lobster Claw from Ottawa's Brookstreet takes a little work, but is a perfect way to impress guests at an informal but stylish dinner party.

Atlantic Crab
Cake

Dayboat, Oyster Bed, PE

This is a fresh twist on an Island crab cake.

4 garlic cloves
1 bunch basil
⅓ cup (90 mL) olive oil
1 cup mayonnaise
salt and pepper
1 x 250 g package Atlantic crab meat
½ bell pepper, finely diced
1 green onion, sliced on a bias
2 tbsp (30 mL) honey
1 cup (250 mL) flour
4 eggs, whisked
panko bread crumbs

Salsa
1 mango
½ bell pepper
¼ small red onion, diced
6 springs of cilantro
¼ cup (65 mL) olive oil

In a food processor, purée garlic, basil and olive oil to make pesto, fold into mayonnaise and season to taste.

Mix crabmeat (all moisture removed), half bell pepper and green onion, incorporate pesto and honey and season to taste.

Form crab mix into cakes and dredge each cake in flour, then in eggs, then in panko crumbs.

For the salsa, chop and mix the mango, bell pepper and red onion. Slice the cilantro and mix together with mango mix, toss in olive oil and season to taste.

Fry crab cakes in oil at 300ºF (150ºC) until golden brown, serve topped with salsa and garnished with a sprig of cilantro.

Malpeque Bay Oyster
Caesar Shooter

Dayboat, Oyster Bed, PE

2 celery stalks
⅓ cup (90 mL) tomato juice
1 cup (250 mL) heavy cream (35% m.f.)
4 Malpeque oysters
celery salt
4 oz (120 mL) Newfoundland vodka
zest of 1 lemon

Cut celery sticks, and make a slit in the middle
half way up each stick. Add tomato juice to
cream, whip to a foam and season. Shuck
oysters, keeping juices.

Rim a champagne glass with celery salt, place an
oyster with its juices in the glass. Add 1 oz
vodka, lemon zest and top with tomato foam.
Slip a stick of celery over the edge of the glass.

Makes 4 drinks.

Seafood
Tasting

Aqua, St. John's, NL

Nothing says Newfoundland better than a seafood tasting. Here we use the famous cod cheeks, which I find almost scallop-like in texture. Halibut and salmon from the very cold Atlantic water is firmer than fish from the West Coast and has more fat.

Cod Cheeks
1 tsp (5 mL) salt
1 tsp (5 mL) black pepper
1 tsp (5 mL) cumin
6 cod cheeks
chickpea flour, for dusting
2 tbsp (30 mL) olive oil

Green Olive Apple Current Salsa
½ lb (240 g) green olives, pitted
½ cup (125 g) apple, peeled and diced
¼ tsp (2 mL) crushed red pepper flakes
1 clove garlic, diced
1 tbsp (15 mL) currants
3 tbsp (45 mL) red wine vinegar
½ cup (125 mL) chopped parsley
¼ cup (65 mL) olive oil
salt

Yields 2 cups (500 mL)

Butter Poached Halibut
1 x 12 oz (360 g) halibut fillet
1 lb (450 g) unsalted butter
1 shallot, finely diced
2 tbsp (30 mL) white wine vinegar
salt and white pepper

Beet Relish
1 cup (250 mL) cooked beets, finely diced
½ cup (125 mL) finely chopped cabbage
1 cup (250 mL) finely chopped apple
½ cup (125 mL) apple cider vinegar
½ cup (125 mL) white sugar
½ tsp (3 mL) salt
½ tsp (3 mL) pepper
1 tbsp 15 (mL) whole-grain mustard

Yields 2 cups (500 mL)

Leek And Black Pepper Crusted Salmon

1 x 12 oz (360 g) salmon fillet

salt and pepper

olive oil, for searing

½ cup (125 mL) finely sliced leeks

salt and coarse black pepper (second amount)

1 tsp (5 mL) lemon juice

1 tsp (5 mL) olive oil

Blueberry Tamari Sauce

2 cups (500 mL) white wine

1 cup (250 mL) corn syrup

1 cup (250 mL) soy sauce

½ cup (125 mL) fresh blueberries

Yields 1 ½ cup (375 mL)

Continued on p. 38

Seafood Tasting
(continued)

Prepare the cod cheeks by mixing salt, pepper and cumin together. Dredge cheeks in chickpea flour and fry in olive oil until golden and crispy. Season with spice mix, set aside and keep warm.

In a medium-sized bowl combine all salsa ingredients and refrigerate.

Cut halibut into six 2 oz (60 g) portions. Over a very low heat melt butter and add shallot, vinegar and seasoning, whisking slowly to keep butter emulsified. When all butter has melted add halibut pieces and cook over a low heat, about 10 to 12 minutes, until halibut is just cooked through.

To make the relish, combine beets, cabbage, apple and vinegar in a pot, stir well, cover and let stand 1 hour. Drain and discard vinegar, add remaining ingredients and bring to a boil. Cool, then refrigerate.

Preheat oven to 450ºF (230ºC). Cut salmon into six 2 oz (60 g) portions and season with salt and pepper. Sear in a hot nonstick pan in olive oil. Mix leeks, salt, black pepper, lemon juice and olive oil together in a small bowl. Place enough of the mixture on each piece of salmon to just cover the top. Cook in oven about 5 minutes, or until salmon is slightly pink in the centre.

To prepare the blueberry sauce, in a pot simmer wine, corn syrup and soy sauce and reduce until it coats the back of a spoon. Add blueberries and cool. Serve at room temperature.

On a rectangular plate, place a generous spoonful of olive salsa with a cod cheek on top. In a straight line place a generous spoonful of beet relish with a piece of halibut on top, followed by the blueberry sauce with a piece of salmon on top.

Serves 6.

Cured Peppered
Halibut

Charlotte Lane Café, Shelburne, NS

If you like lox you'll love this. The principle is the same, but the use of halibut is new. Try to secure Atlantic halibut for this dish, as the flesh is a little firmer than West Coast fish, making it easier to slice.

2 lemons
2 limes
½ cup (125 mL) salt
½ cup (125 mL) brown sugar
3 lb (750 g) halibut filet
black pepper, ground
8 oz (250 g) fresh dill
2 oz (60 g) pecorino
extra virgin olive oil

Cut lemons and limes into thin slices. Mix salt and sugar together. In a large pan place half the lemons, limes and dill in a layer, cover with half the salt mix, place fish on top, cover fish with remaining salt mix, packing it firmly, then layer remaining lemons, limes and dill. Cover with plastic wrap and refrigerate 12 hours. Remove fish from pan, rinse off curing mix and dry fillet well. Sprinkle both sides with a good layer of ground black pepper and slice paper thin.

Serve on a plate, sprinkle with grated pecorino and drizzle with extra virgin olive oil.

Serves 6.

Dungeness Crab
Cakes

Mahle House, Nanaimo, BC

Moist crab cakes with a crisp outer crust are best made using panko breadcrumbs. The saffron aïoli adds a nice floral note to the sweet crabmeat.

1 red pepper, finely diced
1 tbsp (15 mL) butter
1 ½ lb (750 g) Dungeness crab
3 scallions, finely sliced
½ cup (125 mL) panko
¼ cup (65 mL) mayonnaise
3 eggs
flour for dusting
2 cups (500 mL) panko (second amount, for
   breading)
oil for frying
2 tbsp (30 mL) butter

Saffron Aïoli
1 tbsp (15 mL) minced garlic
2 tbsp (30 mL) saffron tea *
1 cup (250 mL) mayonnaise

Sweat red pepper in butter until soft. Cool and add to crab and scallions in a bowl. Add panko to the bowl and toss. Stir in mayonnaise to just bind mixture together. Form mixture into 3-in (7.5-cm) cakes. Lightly beat eggs in a bowl. Dust cakes with flour and dip them in egg and panko. Place on a plate in refrigerator until cakes set and firm a little. Cook cakes in a medium-hot pan with oil and butter until browned and hot in centre.

Stir all aïoli ingredients in a bowl until well combined and colour is blended.

Place a crab cake on each plate and spoon a pool of aïoli on the side garnish with lemon wedges

Serve crab cakes with saffron aïoli

* Saffron tea is threads of saffron steeped in white wine.

Serves 6.

Corn and Crab
Fritters

Tempest Restaurant, Wolfville, NS

The flavours of corn and crab go so well together as they are both sweet in taste. A sprinkle of sea salt seems to intensify the sweetness.

1 cup (250 mL) all-purpose flour
1 cup (250 mL) cornmeal
1 tsp (5 mL) baking powder
salt and pepper
1 large egg
1 egg yolk
1 tbsp (15 mL) melted butter
½ red pepper, chopped
½ yellow pepper, chopped
1 cup (250 mL) corn kernels
1 shallot, chopped
2 cloves garlic, minced
2 tbsp (30 mL) chopped cilantro
1 cup (250 mL) cooked crabmeat
paprika and cayenne to taste
⅔ cup (165 mL) beer

Combine flour, corn meal, baking powder, salt and pepper in a bowl and set aside. In a separate bowl mix egg, egg yolk and melted butter. In a pan over medium heat, sauté red and yellow peppers, corn kernels and shallot in butter 3 minutes. Add garlic, cook 1 minute, remove from heat and cool. Once cooled combine all ingredients together and refrigerate ½ hour.

Half fill a pan with oil and heat to 320°F (160°C). Fry small scoops of batter until golden brown. Remove from oil, drop onto a platter lined with paper towel to absorb excess oil and sprinkle with coarse salt. Serve immediately.

Serves 12.

Poached Lobster Claw, Fiddlehead and
White Truffle Flash, Chèvre and Apricot Twix

Brookstreet, Ottawa, ON

This recipe may appear a little time consuming, but it will be a big hit with your dinner guests. All the components work together, with a complete ying and yang balance.

Fiddlehead and White Truffle Flash

1 tsp (5 mL) minced garlic
½ celery rib, sliced
1 shallot, sliced
4 tsp (20 mL) olive oil
1 tsp (5 mL) white truffle oil
8 oz (250 g) fiddleheads
¾ cup (190 mL) vegetable stock
5 oz (150 mL) heavy cream (35% m.f.)
16 oz (250 g) baby spinach leaves

Chèvre and Apricot Twix

3 phyllo sheets
3 oz (90mL) clarified butter, melted
5 oz (150 g) chèvre, creamed
1 apricot, quartered

Buttered Lobster Claw

4 lobster claws
3 oz (90 mL) butter
¼ cup (65 mL) heavy cream (35% m.f.)
salt and pepper

In a skillet over medium heat, sauté garlic, celery and shallots in olive oil and white truffle oil until transparent, add fiddleheads and cook 5 minutes. Add vegetable stock and bring to a boil, then add cream and return to a boil and simmer 3 minutes, or until reduced by one-third. Add baby spinach leaves, set aside and keep warm.

Lay a sheet of phyllo on worktop, and using a pastry brush paint entire sheet with clarified butter. Repeat process, laying sheets one on top of another until three sheets are applied. Cut phyllo into 4 lengths. Place a piece of chèvre and apricot on each length and roll up each length like a spring roll. Bake phyllo twix in a 350°F (180°C) oven 10 minutes, or until golden brown.

Cook lobster claws in a pot of well-salted boiling water 6 minutes. Transfer claws to an ice bath 6 minutes to stop the cooking process. Deshell claws. In a sauté pan melt butter, add claws and cream and cook until reduced to a saucelike consistency. Adjust seasoning with salt and pepper.

Divide fiddlehead flash in the centre of the serving plates and top with a lobster claw. Place chèvre twix between jaws of claw as though it is holding the twix. Dress with a touch of butter cream that was used to cook lobster. Serve immediately.

Serves 4.

Pickerel Cheeks Poached
in Tomato Consommé

Little Britt Inn, Britt, ON

Cheeks are the little jewels of the pickerel. Just like the cheeks of the codfish, they burst with flavour and have a great texture. The sweetness of the meat pairs well with the acid of the tomato consommé, and is counterbalanced with the ouzo.

12 plum tomatoes
¼ cup (65 ml) olive oil
1 large onion
1 leek
4 cloves garlic
1 large carrot
1 fennel bulb
4 cups (1 L) chicken stock
good pinch saffron
salt and pepper
1 oz (30 mL) ouzo
24 pickerel cheeks

Preheat oven to 375°F (190°C). Place tomatoes in an ovenproof dish, drizzle with olive oil and roast 40 minutes. While they are roasting dice onion, leek, garlic, carrot and fennel, reserving fennel fronds for garnish. Place diced vegetables in a pot, drizzle with oil and cook gently until tender. Add chicken stock and tomatoes, bring to a boil and simmer 20 minutes. Pass mixture through a food mill. Reheat, adding saffron, salt and pepper. Simmer and add ouzo. Place cheeks in sauce and poach to required doneness. Carefully remove cheeks, divide them among plates and ladle sauce over top. Garnish with fennel fronds.

Serves 6.

Tom Yam
Goong

Brookstreet, Ottawa, ON

This soup is quick to make and, like most Asian-influenced dishes, prides itself on clean fresh flavours with sweet, salty and sour elements.

4 cups (1 L) chicken stock
2 stems lemon grass
2 in (5 cm) galangal
2 kaffir lime leaves
8 shrimp
½ oz (15 g) tom yum paste
2 shallots, sliced
juice of 1 lime
2 tbsp (50 mL) fish sauce
¼ cup (65 ml) cilantro

In a medium-sized pot bring stock to a boil, add lemon grass, galangal and lime leaves and simmer 15 minutes. Add shrimp, tom yum paste and shallots and continue to simmer 3 minutes. Add lime juice and fish sauce to taste. The soup should have a spicy, sour slightly salty taste.

Divide soup into 4 small bowls, garnish with cilantro and serve.

Serves 4.

Langoustines Simply Roasted with Espelette Chili,
Tomatoes and Cured Fennel with Basil, Tomato Sabayon, Accompanied by a Small Salad

Signatures, Ottawa, ON

This recipe clearly shows how the simplest of ingredients let the true tastes shine. Langoustines, also known as scampi, are best if you can find ones from Iceland. The cold water makes these deep-sea lobster tails sweet.

10 langoustines
1 tsp (5 mL) Espelette chili*
2 tbsp (30 mL) extra virgin olive oil
pinch of salt
5 oz (150 g) micro greens
3 tbsp (45 mL) olive oil
1 tbsp (15 mL) lemon juice

Concassée of Tomatoes, Fennel and Basil
4 red tomatoes
sea salt
pepper
2 tbsp (30 mL) olive oil
1 tbsp (15 mL) capers
½ tsp (3 mL) ground coriander
1 sprig fresh basil, leaves removed and finely shredded
1 bulb fennel
1 sprig fresh thyme
1 clove garlic

Yields 1 ½ cups (375 mL)

Tomato sauce
3 red tomatoes
½ small onion, finely diced
1 tbsp (15 mL) olive oil
1 clove garlic, finely chopped

Yields ½ cup (125 mL)

Sabayon de Tomate
2 egg yolks
½ cup (125 mL) tomato sauce

Yields ½ cup (125 mL)

Shell langoustines, leaving tails attached. Using a small knife, make a light incision down the back in order to remove intestine. Toss with chili, olive oil and salt, cover and refrigerate until needed.

To make the concassée, peel and seed tomatoes and arrange in an ovenproof dish. Season with salt and pepper and lightly sprinkle with olive oil. Place in a pre-heated 250°F (120°C) oven for 30 minutes. Remove and chop finely. Mix capers, ground coriander and basil together and set aside. Cut fennel bulb into small dice and place over medium heat in olive oil with thyme and garlic. Cook approximately 5 minutes. Drain fennel, making sure to remove garlic and thyme. Add roast tomatoes and the caper mix.

Continued on p. 48

Langoustines Simply Roasted (Continued)

For the tomato sauce, peel and seed tomatoes and purée in a blender until smooth. In a small pot gently cook onion in olive oil until soft without colouring. Add garlic and tomato purée. Allow to reduce until thick, about 30 minutes.

Prepare the sabayon by heating a hot-water bath to simmering. Place egg yolks into a heatproof bowl and add 1 tbsp (15 mL) water. Place in the hot-water bath and whisk until light yellow in colour and the whisk leaves a trail in mixture. Gently fold in tomato sauce, being careful not to over mix and break the emulsion.

Sear langoustines in olive oil. Lightly toss micro greens in olive oil and lemon juice.

In a shallow soup bowl, place concassée in the centre (use a small circle mould if desired). Pour sabayon around and then arrange langoustines on top, two per plate. Finish with a bouquet of salad on top.

*Espelette chili is a mild seasoning that can be found in specialty gourmet shops. If unavailable use paprika, being careful to use just enough to lightly dust langoustine.

Serves 5.

Grilled Spigola (Mediterranean Sea Bass)
with Herbed Salad and White Balsamic Vinaigrette

Il Mulino, Toronto, ON

Sea bass is a great, firm fish that holds up to several cooking styles. Here it is paired with a somewhat new vinegar, white balsamic. It is different in taste to the regular dark vinegar, and more tart.

4 spigola fillets
salt and pepper
2 tbsp (30 mL) olive oil
1 cup (250 mL) parsley
1 cup (250 mL) chervil leaves
1 cup (250 mL) mint leaves
1 cup (250 mL) basil leaves
1 cup (250 mL) chives, cut in half
1 cup (250 mL) arugula
1 cup (250 mL) chopped heirloom tomatoes
4 tbsp (60 mL) extra virgin olive oil
1 tbsp (15 mL) white balsamic vinegar
lava salt

Season spigola with salt and pepper, lightly oil and grill until desired doneness. Mix herbs and tomatoes in a bowl and drizzle with extra virgin olive oil and vinegar to make vinaigrette.

Arrange grilled fish on a plate, top with herb salad and vinaigrette and finish with a sprinkling of lava salt.

Serves 4.

Sautéed Finlayson Arm Spotted Prawn
and Truffled Sooke Rabbit, Boudin Blanc with Black Truffle and Watercress Emulsion

Aerie Resort, Malahat, BC

Spotted prawns are caught in the seafood-rich waters of the West Coast. There is a very small window of opportunity to get them, and they sell very quickly. Together with the sausage they make a great twist on "surf and turf."

Boudin Blanc
1 ½ oz (45 g) bread
3 tbsp (45 mL) milk (3.25% m.f.)
5 tbsp (75 mL) heavy cream (35% m.f.)
4 tbsp (60 mL) black truffle oil
2 tsp (10 mL) cornstarch
1 egg white
1 tsp (5 mL) salt
black pepper
3 oz (90 g) rabbit
2 oz (60 g) pork jaw
2 oz (60 g) chicken
2 oz (60 g) foie gras
1 shallot
½ oz (15 g) black truffle
sausage casing
½ bunch watercress

juice of ½ lemon
1 tbsp (15 mL) grainy mustard
4 tbsp (60 mL) black truffle oil
4 tbsp (60 mL) grape seed oil
2 tbsp (30 mL) sherry vinegar
12 spotted prawn tails
olive oil
salt and pepper
micro greens, for garnish

Make the boudin blanc by soaking bread with milk, cream and black truffle oil. In a bowl mix cornstarch, egg white, salt and pepper together and reserve. Grind all meats together with shallot and black truffle. In a food processor add meats and bread mix and process until well blended. Transfer mixture to a bowl and incorporate cornstarch mix, using a spatula. Using the sausage skin, make mixture into 2 oz (60 g) sausages. Poach at 180°F (90°C) 25 to 30 minutes. Cool in ice and reserve.

Remove and discard stems from watercress.
Wash leaves and blanch in boiling salted water
10 seconds. Cool, squeeze excess water out and
reserve. In a blender, incorporate lemon juice,
grain mustard, truffle oil, grape seed oil and
sherry vinegar. Add watercress to blender and
purée. Set aside. If watercress makes the
emulsion taste too bitter, add a touch of honey.

Peel prawns. Sauté boudin blanc with a little
olive oil until golden brown. Add prawns to the
same frying pan and sauté about 2 minutes.
Spoon 1 tbsp of watercress dressing on a plate.
Stack 3 prawns and 1 boudin blanc on the
dressing. Top the stack with micro greens.

Serves 4.

Salmon Poached in Olive Oil
with Arugula

Casa Bella, Gananoque, ON

You might think that poaching in oil would make the fish oily. In fact poaching in a high-quality olive oil seals in the moisture and adds a slight nutty flavour and aroma to the fish.

12 oz (360 g) Atlantic salmon fillet
2 cups (500 mL) extra virgin olive oil
2 garlic cloves
zest of 1 lemon
4 sprigs thyme
1 to 2 bunches arugula
juice of ½ lemon
grey sea salt

Slice salmon on the bias into four 3 oz (90 g) portions. Season with salt. In a shallow pot just big enough to hold salmon portions in a single layer, heat olive oil, garlic, lemon zest and thyme sprigs to 155°F (68°C).

Place salmon portions in hot oil, which will cool down with the addition of the fish, and cook at 145°F (62°C) 10 minutes. Salmon will be just cooked. Be careful to keep temperature below 150°F (65°C) or beads of white fat will start to appear.

Remove salmon from oil and arrange one portion on each of four plates. Toss arugula with a squirt of lemon juice and a pinch of salt. Pile arugula beside salmon. Drizzle a little poaching oil over salmon and arugula and season with a pinch of grey sea salt.

Serves 4.

Island Style Salmon
Sashimi

Dayboat, Oyster Bed, PE

This is a great twist on Japanese sashimi using Island ingredients.

zest of 1 lime
zest of 1 lemon
juice of 2 limes
½ to ¾ tsp (2 to 3 mL) pickled ginger liquid
1 x 250 g fresh Atlantic salmon fillet
1 PEI russet potato
oil, for frying
salt and pepper
1 tbsp (25 mL) horseradish sauce
4 tbsp (100 mL) sour cream
1 lime
1 lemon
1 pink grapefruit
2 chives

To make marinade, finely chop lemon and lime zest and mix with lime juice. Incorporate pickled ginger liquid.

Slice salmon fillet in half and cut into ⅛-in (3-mm) thick slices lengthwise. Place on a baking sheet lined with parchment paper. Brush salmon with marinade on both sides and refrigerate 2 hours.

Slice potato on a mandoline into pieces the size of potato chips. Pat dry, fry in hot oil at 300°F (150°C) and place on a sheet of paper towel. Season.

Fold horseradish into sour cream to make a crème fraiche.

Segment lime, lemon and grapefruit, then cut segments into quarters and halves, depending on size. Finely chop chives and keep separate.

Roll up salmon slices, place on potato crisps, add a small portion of fruit on top and drizzle with horseradish crème fraiche. Garnish with chives.

Serves 4.

Roast Celery Root Soup
with Caramelized Digby Scallops

Chives Canadian Bistro, Halifax, NS

Searing the scallops in a hot pan brings out their natural sugars. The sweet flavours from the ocean balance nicely with the celery root from the earth.

1 large onion, diced
2 ribs celery, diced
2 tbsp (30 mL) canola oil
2 peeled and roasted celery roots
8 cups (2 L) chicken stock
½ cup (125 mL) butter
1 cup (250 mL) heavy cream (35% m.f.)
12 x 10-20 count sea scallops
3 tbsp (45 mL) canola, peanut or vegetable oil
salt and pepper to taste

In a large pot sweat onion and celery in oil. Add roasted celery roots, cover with stock and bring to a boil. Simmer 1 hour. Purée soup in a food processor or blender until smooth. Return to pot, add butter and cream.

Heat another pan until very warm. Add the oil and place each scallop carefully onto the pan so it sits on a flat side. Do not move the pan for 1 to 2 minutes to allow the scallop to sear properly. Turn once and finish cooking for only 30 seconds on the second side. Season with a little salt and pepper.

Season and divide between 4 bowls, placing 3 scallops in each bowl, served seared side up.

Serves 4.

Diver Digby Scallops
with Madras Curry Sauce

Onyx, Halifax, NS

The Asian influence in this dish shines through with the lime leaves and coconut. The richness of the scallops is softened by the fresh citrus taste from the lime leaves, and is brought to a new level with the sweet curry.

4 tbsp (60 mL) canola oil
½ cup (125 mL) peeled and chopped shallots
3 ½ tbsp (50 mL) curry paste
1 tsp (5 mL) curry powder, "Madras Curry" brand
¼ cup (65 mL) dark rum
½ cup (125 mL) coconut milk
1 stalk lemon grass, finely chopped
2 kaffir lime leaves, chopped
2 tbsp (30mL) maple syrup
kosher salt and freshly ground pepper
siracha (chili sauce), to taste
¼ bunch cilantro, chopped
4 x U-10 scallops

In a small saucepan on medium-high heat, pour 2 tablespoons of oil and sauté shallots until transparent. Add curry paste and powder and sauté until aroma fills the air. Deglaze with rum and add coconut milk, lemon grass, lime leaves and maple syrup and bring to a boil. Reduce the heat and simmer 15 minutes or until curry sauce thickens. Remove from the heat and adjust flavour with salt and freshly ground pepper, siracha (if you like it hot) and fresh cilantro.

In a separate sauté pan, pour remaining oil and place the pan on high heat. When oil is smoking hot, quickly season scallops and sear them both sides, until golden brown outside and plump and juicy inside.

Serve scallops with curry sauce.

Serves 4.

Seared Scallops
with a Carrot Juice Reduction

Little Britt Inn, Britt, ON

The natural sugar in the carrots adds just the
sweetness needed to help cut the richness of
the scallops. Perfectly paired, the butter in the
velvety smooth sauce accents the buttery texture
of the scallops.

24 large scallops
5 lb (2.5 kg) carrots
1 tbsp (15 mL butter)

Peel and juice carrots, and reduce juice by one-
half in a large pot over medium-low heat,
skimming foam from the top as juice reduces. In
a heavy-bottomed skillet sear scallops, remove
and keep warm, tented with foil wrap. Pour
juice into pan and simmer to reduce until syrupy.
Whisk in butter.

Spoon a pool of sauce in the middle of each
plate and top with 3 scallops.

Serves 8.

Agnolotti Pasta, p.66

Mains — Fish, Fowl and Vegetarian

The flavours here are bold but appealing, and the focus is on quality, freshness and being as local as possible. The ingredients are often very simple, like the fresh pasta and mushrooms in the Fettuccini con Funghi from Burlington's 1505 North — or more complex, like the delicious Duck Breast with Honey and Marsala from Shelburne's Charlotte Lane Café, with its rich ingredients and flavourful accompaniments. Any of these dishes will work well as a main course or as a component of a magnificent multi-course meal.

Black Bean
Omelette

Pacific Rim Grille, Coquitlam, BC

A great egg preparation for a lacto-ova-vegetarian. The beans add lots of good protein, and the goat cheese adds a soft creamy tanginess.

Bean Purée
6 cups (1.5 L) black beans, soaked 12 hours
1 rib celery, diced
½ large onion, diced
1 tbsp (15 mL) garlic, chopped
10 cups (2.5 L) vegetable stock
2 oz (60 g) canned chipotle
salt and pepper

Salsa
2 tomatoes
1 small red onion
½ medium green pepper
2 tbsp (30 mL) chopped cilantro
2 dashes Tabasco sauce
juice of ½ lime
salt and pepper

Mint Chutney
4 cups (1 L) packed mint leaves
1 tsp (5 mL) chopped garlic
1 small red onion, diced
½ cup (125 mL) water
1 cup (250 mL) sour cream

Omelette
½ shallot, finely diced
½ tsp (2 mL) chopped garlic
1 tbsp (15 mL) canola oil
bean purée
3 oz (90 g) goat cheese
tortilla chips, to garnish

In a large pot cook beans, celery, onion, and garlic in enough stock to cover, until beans are tender. Add more stock as needed during cooking. Remove from heat and cool. Purée with chipotle until smooth. Season to taste.

Prepare salsa by dicing vegetables and placing in a bowl with cilantro. Add Tabasco, lime juice, and salt and pepper to taste.

For the mint chutney, place mint, garlic, onion and water in the bowl of a food processor, and pulse until coarse. Stir in sour cream.

In a large, heavy-bottomed skillet sauté shallot and garlic in oil. Add bean purée and cook, stirring frequently until beans start to get crusty. Flatten with a spatula, place goat cheese in centre of omelette and fold over. Remove from the pan and keep warm in the oven while you make 3 more omelettes.

Place one omelette on each plate, garnish with salsa, chutney and tortilla chips.

Serves 4.

Grana Padano and Ricotta Gnocchi
with Roasted Chestnut, Sage and Truffle-Scented Brown Butter, Grana Crisp

Il Mulino, Toronto, ON

Gnocchi are little dumplings generally made from potato. Here we have one made with ricotta cheese. They are much lighter and pair extremely well with the chestnuts that abound in northern Italy.

1 cup (250 mL) grated Grana Padano
2 cups (500 mL) fresh ricotta
¼ cup (60 mL) all-purpose flour
½ tsp (2 mL) nutmeg
1 cup (250 mL) grated Grana Padano (second amount)
2 tbsp (30 mL) butter
¼ cup (60 mL) white truffle oil
1 cup (250 mL) roasted chestnuts
2 sage leaves

In a mixing bowl combine Grana Padano, ricotta, flour and nutmeg. Mix to consistency of light dough. Cut and roll into gnocchi using the back of a fork to make shallow grooves.

On a baking sheet lined with parchment paper make 4 circular mounds of grated cheese, keeping them about 3 in (7.5 cm) apart. Bake at 400°F (200°C) until golden. Remove from oven and place individually over the back of a small steel bowl until cheese crisps form the bowl's shape.

Bring a large pot of well-salted water to a roiling boil and cook gnocchi until they float.

In a pan over high heat, heat butter and truffle oil until brown, then add chestnuts and sage and continue to heat until warmed.

Remove gnocchi from pot and add to sauce. Divide gnocchi onto plates and set a cheese crisp to the side.

Serves 4.

Fettuccini
con Funghi

1505 North, Burlington, ON

Mushrooms, the sponges of the forest, love to soak up any flavours you can give them. Here the addition of balsamic vinegar lends a sweet flavour to complement the richness of the mushrooms and cream.

1 lb (500 g) fettuccine
6 oz (180 g) wild mushrooms
1 tbsp (15 mL) olive oil
2 oz (60 g) red wine
1 oz (30 mL) balsamic vinegar
6 oz (180 mL) heavy cream (35% m.f.)
2 oz (60 mL) demi-glace
1 grilled chicken breast, diced
2 basil leaves, chopped
salt and pepper
parmigiano cheese, to taste

In a large pot of well-salted boiling water cook pasta al dente.

While pasta is cooking, make the sauce. In a large pan over high heat, sauté mushrooms in oil. When mushrooms begin to soften pour in wine and reduce to a glaze. Add vinegar and reduce by half. Pour in cream and demi-glace and add diced chicken and basil. Season with salt and pepper, add cooked pasta and toss.

Divide between four plates and sprinkle with parmigiano.

Serves 4.

Ravioli Ripieno Anitra
e Gorgonzola con Fico

La Perla, Dartmouth, NS

This recipe has become a favourite in my cooking classes. The strong, rich flavours and textures are seduced by the sauce elements. The orange liqueur I use is Grand Marnier, brandy based with bitter orange. I find that the fresh orange takes a bite out of the rich filling.

Basic Fresh Pasta
3 cups (750 mL) all-purpose flour
1 tbsp (15 mL) salt
5 large eggs
1 tbsp (15 mL) olive oil

Makes 12 ravioli

Filling
2 duck breasts, roasted
12 dried black mission figs
4 oz (120 g) mascarpone
2 oz (60 g) Gorgonzola

Sauce
2 oranges
1 oz. orange liqueur
1 cup (250 mL) demi-glace
parmigiano cheese to taste

The "well" method of making pasta is the oldest and most traditional way. On a wooden surface make a mound with flour and salt, then create a well in the middle of the mound. Add eggs and olive oil and slowly incorporate the flour, taking care not to break the sides of the mound. Once flour and eggs are mixed, start the kneading process by continually folding and turning dough. Wrap with a dishtowel and let rest ½ hour.

In the bowl of a food processor blend duck, figs and cheeses together to make the filling. Place in a pastry bag and set aside. Roll pasta dough through a pasta roller, working through the settings until you reach the thinnest. Make certain you have enough for 24 pieces. Line a ravioli form with dough and add filling. Cook in well-salted boiling water 4 minutes. Drain.

Into a large pan, add juice and zest of oranges, then add liqueur and demi-glace. Reduce and simmer with pasta. Serve and sprinkle with parmigiano.

Serves 6.

Agnolotti Pasta
(Pasta Stuffed with Walnuts, Prunes, Spinach and Gorgonzola, Served with a Squash Sauce Scented with Orange)

Charlotte Lane Café, Shelburne, NS

A symphony of taste is the best way to describe the action in this pasta. With each bite you get a different feel, just like the different sections of the orchestra.

Pasta
8 oz (250 mL) ricotta
2 oz (60 g) Gorgonzola
2 oz (60 g) prunes
1 oz (30 g) walnuts
2 oz (60 g) cooked spinach
1 lb (500 g) fresh pasta

Sauce
juice of 2 oranges
zest of 2 oranges
3 lb (1.5 kg) butternut squash
2 cups (500 mL) whipping cream
½ tsp (2 mL) ground nutmeg
salt and pepper
parmigiano cheese, to taste

In a large bowl mix cheeses, prunes, walnuts and spinach together to make the filling. Roll out pasta dough paper-thin and cut into 36 3 x 3-in (7.5 x 7.5-cm) squares. Divide filling between half the pasta squares, cover each one with another square and seal well. Set aside.

For the sauce, zest and juice the oranges, retaining the squeezed portions. Peel and steam squash with retained squeezed oranges until very soft. Discard squeezed oranges and purée squash in a food processor. Place puréed squash in a large pot and add cream, juice, zest, nutmeg and seasoning.

Cook pasta 4 minutes. Place a generous amount of sauce on the plates and serve pasta on top. Sprinkle with parmigiano.

Serves 6.

North Shore Halibut
with Island Lobster

Dayboat, Oyster Bed, PE

This dish captures the essence of fresh Island ingredients, and is perfect for entertaining guests on a summer day.

20 PEI fingerling potatoes
¾ cup (180 g) mascarpone cheese
½ cup (125 g) butter
2 green onions, cut on a bias
salt and pepper
½ cup (125 g) sugar snap peas
2 shallots, sliced
½ cup (125 mL) white wine
1 cup (250 mL) heavy cream (35% m.f.)
salt and pepper
zest of 1 lemon
juice of 2 lemons
1 x 1 ¼ lb (625 g) lobster
4 x 5 oz (150 g) halibut fillets
1 cup (250 L) white wine (second amount)
½ cup (125 mL) fish stock (or water)
¼ cup (65 g) whipped butter
flour, for dusting
olive oil, for frying
fresh market vegetables

Place potatoes in a pot of cool, salted water and bring to a boil. Cook until fork tender, strain and smash with mascarpone, butter, green onions and seasoning. The mix should look rustic, not mashed.

Boil peas 2 minutes, shock in cool water, strain and purée to consistency of baby food (they may need a little water). In a pot, sweat shallots until they are translucent, deglaze with ½ cup (125 mL) white wine and reduce by two-thirds. Once reduced, slowly add cream while whisking to avoid curdling. Reduce until cream coats the back of a spoon, whisk in pea purée and season to taste. Place lobster in a pot of boiling water and boil 12 minutes. Cool and de-shell, set aside claws, then chop the tail and knuckles and incorporate into cream sauce.

Toss halibut in lemon zest and place in a 2-in (5-cm) deep tray. Add 1 cup (250 mL) white wine white wine, lemon juice and fish stock (water is permissible), until halibut is one-quarter covered. Top each fillet with a teaspoon of whipped butter and season. Cover tray with foil and bake at 375°F (190°C), 10 minutes.

Form potato mix into cakes (hockey puck size),
dust with flour and pan fry on medium heat
with olive oil. Once browned place potato cakes
on the plate and top with halibut. Place a
lobster claw on top of fish and finish with
lobster cream sauce. Serve with in-season
market vegetables.

Serves 4.

Tournedos de Fletan
Halibut with Citrus Turnip, Mashed Potato and Lobster Sauce

Signatures, Ottawa, ON

A true taste of French cuisine: simple ingredients combined to raise the flavour level to unbelievable heights. A truly rich course that can be well enjoyed with a crisp Sauvignon Blanc.

Halibut

1 lb (500 g) halibut fillet
fine sea salt
2 tbsp (30 mL) olive oil
1 clove garlic
1 sprig thyme

Citrus Turnips

zest of 1 lemon
2 oz (60 g) sugar
10 mini-turnips
2 oz (60 g) butter

Mashed Potato

1 lb (500 g) fingerling potatoes
7 oz (200 g) butter, cut into small pieces
7 oz (200 g) heavy cream (35% m.f.), heated
2 oz (60 g) porcini mushrooms, sliced

Lobster Sauce

1 tbsp (15 mL) olive oil
2 lobster bodies
2 shallots, chopped
1 onion, chopped
1 rib celery, chopped
1 carrot, chopped
2 oz (60 mL) cognac
2 fresh tomatoes
2 cloves garlic
3 tarragon fronds
1 bouquet garni
1 cup (250 mL) dry white wine
1 tsp (5 mL) tomato paste
2 cups (500 mL) chicken stock
salt and pepper
pinch of cayenne pepper
3 oz (90 mL) heavy cream (35% m.f.)

Cut halibut into ten equal pieces and tie them in twos, one on top of the other, with string. Refrigerate until ready to cook.

For the citrus turnips, blanch lemon zest three times to remove any bitterness. Add sugar and enough water to cover. Candy gently over low heat, about 30 minutes. Drain and set aside. Peel turnips and slice thinly into rounds. Cook gently in butter over low heat with zest of lemon. Season to taste.

For mashed potatoes, boil fingerling potatoes in salted water until tender. Peel and crush through a food mill. Add butter, piece by piece, then add hot cream. Sauté mushrooms in butter and stir into crushed potatoes. Set aside and keep warm.

To make lobster sauce, heat oil in a heavy pan and add lobster bodies. Once they have turned bright red, add vegetables and mix well. Add cognac and flambé. Add tomatoes, garlic, tarragon, bouquet garni, white wine, tomato paste and chicken stock. The lobster bodies should just be covered with liquid; if not, add enough water to cover. Season with salt and pepper and a pinch of cayenne pepper. Cover and cook over medium heat, 30 minutes. Add cream and reduce until thick enough to coat the back of a spoon, or to desired consistency. Strain through a fine sieve, adjust seasoning and keep warm. Just before serving emulsify with a hand mixer.

Season fish parcels with fine sea salt and sear in a sauté pan in olive oil with a clove of garlic and a sprig of thyme. To keep fish moist, the centre should remain opaque.

Make a comma of mashed potato on the plate. Arrange fish in the centre and place turnips in a line. Spoon emulsified lobster sauce over halibut.

Serves 5.

1505 Shrimp

1505 North, Burlington, ON

Some of the most-loved dishes from any country in the world have their origins in peasant food. People have always come up with imaginative ways to use everything. In this dish it's the use of bread.

2 tbsp (30 mL) olive oil
2 cloves garlic, chopped
1 small red onion, sliced
24 large shrimp (21 to 25 count)
2 oz (60 mL) brandy
4 slices prosciutto
½ cup (125 mL) crushed tomatoes

1 cup (250 mL) heavy cream (35% m.f.)
6 basil leaves, julienned
salt and pepper
4 slices country bread

In a large frying pan heat oil, garlic and onion over high heat. Add shrimp and cook 30 seconds. Flambé with brandy, add prosciutto, tomatoes and cream and reduce by half. Add basil leaves and salt and pepper. While sauce reduces, grill bread and place a piece on each plate. Divide shrimp over bread and pour sauce over.

Serves 4.

Sesame-Crusted Tuna
with Spicy Green Celery Jus

Teatro, Calgary, AB

The lean tuna needs only a short cooking, which leaves a meaty texture. The celery jus — with a hint of heat — marries well with the mix.

Sesame Tuna
1 egg
2 tbsp (30 mL) water
1 cup (250 mL) sesame seeds
8 oz (250 g) tuna loin, cleaned of fat and
   trimmed
2 tbsp (30 mL) olive oil

Spicy Green Celery Jus
4 celery stalks
olive oil
1 wedge lemon
Tabasco sauce
micro greens, for garnish

Whisk egg lightly with water. Place sesame seeds in a flat pan. Roll tuna around in egg mixture and then in sesame seeds to coat loin on all sides. In a pan of hot oil over medium-high heat, carefully place loin and fry until sesame seeds brown, then turn onto another side, turning down the heat. Finish browning all sides. Tuna is best served rare, so the loin should not be left in a hot pan for too long.

Juice celery stalks in an electric juicer. Add just enough olive oil to thicken juice slightly. Squeeze juice of lemon wedge into mix and add a couple of drops of Tabasco. Adjust to taste.

Slice tuna into 4 portions and place on plate. Spoon celery jus beside tuna. Garnish with a little salad of micro greens.

Serves 8.

Big Eye Tuna Tartare,
Caramelized Banana Lady Fingers and Preserved Black Bean Bouillon

Brookstreet, Ottawa, ON

When buying tuna to serve raw, try to secure Toro grade. This is the most prized cut, from the belly area of the fish. The fat in the fish gives the feel and richness that makes it so divine.

Big Eye Tuna Tartare

10 oz (300 g) tuna, sushi grade
1 oz (30 g) shallots, finely diced
1 tsp (5 mL) minced ginger
1 tsp (5 mL) mustard
5 chives, finely cut
juice of 1 lime
Maldon sea salt
black pepper

Caramelized Banana Lady Fingers

2 bananas
2 oz (60 g) butter unsalted
1 oz (30 g) sugar
4 spring rolls sheets

Preserved Black Bean Bouillon

1 tbsp (15 mL) fish sauce
½ cup (125 mL) chicken stock
2 tbsp (30 mL) mirin
1 oz (30 g) preserved black beans

1 avocado for plate assembly

Cut tuna into small dice. In a stainless steel bowl add tuna, shallots, ginger, mustard, chives and lime juice. Adjust seasoning with salt and pepper.

Peel and cut bananas lengthwise. In a frying pan over medium-high heat, sauté bananas with butter and sugar until golden brown. They should remain firm to the touch. Reserve, cool and refrigerate. Lay a soft spring roll sheet on the worktop in a diamond shape with one corner nearest you. Place one piece of banana in centre of spring roll sheet, leaving approximately 1 ¼ in (3 cm) on each side. Hold the corner closest to you and fold it over filling. Fold both left and right corners and roll up tightly, ensuring there are no air pockets in roll.

In a sauce pot combine fish sauce, chicken stock, mirin and preserved black bean. Bring to a boil and simmer 4 minutes. Remove from heat and allow bouillon to cool to room temperature.

Mash avocado and place a small spoonful in the centre of the plate to act as a holding compound. Deep fry spring rolls to a golden brown, cut each in half, about 3 in (7 cm) in length and place on avocado. Place 4 round forms on plates and spoon tuna tartar into the forms using a spoon to pack it lightly. Spoon the bouillon onto the plate and serve immediately.

Serves 4.

Nova Scotia Duck Breast
with Flageolets

Chives Bistro, Halifax, NS

Flageolet beans have a delicate flavour that goes well with other ingredients. They come in different colours. I like to use white for the colour contrast in the sauce with the tomatoes.

4 boneless duck breasts
3 slices bacon
½ leek, white part only
1 clove garlic
7 oz (210 g) canned flageolets, drained
½ cup (125 mL) grape tomatoes halved
2 tbsp (30 mL) chopped sage
1 oz (30 mL) red wine
2 tbsp (30 mL) olive oil
salt and pepper to taste

Using a sharp knife score skin and fat of duck to help render the fat during cooking.

Roast duck breast, skin side down until desired doneness. Let rest 5 minutes before slicing.

In a large pot over medium heat sauté bacon, leek and garlic until translucent. Turn heat to high and add beans, tomatoes and sage. Cook 2 minutes and add wine and check for seasoning.

Divide bean mixture onto 4 plates and fan sliced duck over. Drizzle with olive oil.

Serves 4.

Petto d'Anatra con Miele e Marsala
Duck Breast with Honey and Marsala Glace with Rosemary Roasted Potato and Broccoli and Cauliflower Cheese Flan

Charlotte Lane Café, Shelburne, NS

Generally game birds are prepared using a sweet component. Here we have Marsala, a fortified wine, and a hint of honey for emphasis. The rosemary takes the edge off the sweetness.

6 boneless duck breasts

Spice Mix for Duck
1 tbsp (15 mL) each of:
salt
pepper
paprika
curry powder
thyme
mustard powder
sage

Sauce
12 oz (360 g) demi-glace
4 oz (120 g) Marsala
1 oz (30 g) honey
2 shallots, chopped
2 cloves garlic
2 sprigs rosemary
2 oz (60 g) butter

Vegetable Flan
10 oz (300 g) cauliflower
10 oz (300 g) broccoli
4 eggs
3 oz (100 mL) heavy cream (35% m.f.)
2 oz (60 g) pecorino
1 tsp (5 mL) paprika
1 tsp (5 mL) nutmeg
salt and pepper

Roast Potatoes
12 baby red potatoes
2 cloves garlic, minced
2 tsp (10 mL) paprika
2 sprigs rosemary
salt and pepper

Season duck breasts with the combined spice mix. Roast duck in an oven at 375°F (190°C) about 20 minutes, until cooked medium.

Place all sauce ingredients except butter in a pot and reduce by one-half over medium-high heat. Remove rosemary, whisk in butter and keep warm.

For the flan, preheat oven to 325°F (165°C). Cook cauliflower and broccoli in a steamer until very soft. Whisk eggs, cream, cheese, spices and seasoning together. Purée vegetables in blender until smooth and mix with egg mixture. Grease small individual ramekins, fill three-quarters full with mixture and bake in oven in a water bath, about 20 to 25 minutes.

Roast baby red potatoes with garlic, paprika, rosemary, salt and pepper until golden crisp.

Slice duck thinly and serve fanned on a pool of sauce with flan and roast potatoes.

Serves 6.

Duck Confit
Agnolotti

Grosvenor's, Southampton, ON

The cooking technique for confit is similar to braising, but the liquid used for confit is duck fat. The duck is well seasoned with salt, allowed to sit for two days then poached in the fat. Today the home chef can purchase the finished product, making life much easier.

Pasta dough
1 ½ cup (375 mL) all-purpose flour
2 large eggs
1 large yolk
½ tbsp (7 mL) salt
1 tsp (5 mL) olive oil

Filling
2 prepared confit duck legs
2 small shallots, diced finely
1 tbsp (15 mL) olive oil
⅓ cup (80 mL) Maderia wine
¼ cup (60 mL) demi-glace
1 tbsp (15 mL) thyme leaves
1 tbsp (15 mL) chopped chervil

Cauliflower Purée
1 cauliflower
1 tbsp (15 mL) butter
1 medium onion, diced
2 cups (500 mL) milk (3.25% m.f.)
2 cups (500 mL) water
salt and pepper

Leeks
3 leeks (white and light green parts)
1 tbsp (15 mL) butter (second amount)
1 cup (250 mL) chicken stock (or water)

extra butter or warm truffle oil, to serve

Place all pasta ingredients in a food processor and pulse until dough forms. Remove and hand knead until smooth. Set aside.

To make filling, shred duck meat from the bone and sauté in oil in a pan with shallots, 2 minutes. Deglaze pan with Maderia and demi-glace, add thyme and chervil and simmer until thick and sticky. Remove from heat and cool completely.

Roll pasta dough through a pasta roller to the thinnest setting, cut 18 large circles from dough. Place a small spoonful of filling in the centre of each, brush edges with water and fold over to seal, making half-moon shapes. Set aside.

For the purée, coarsely chop cauliflower and sauté with butter and onion. Add milk and water and simmer until very soft. Strain excess liquid and reserve. Place cauliflower and onion in food processor and purée until smooth, adding some of reserved liquid if needed. Season with salt and pepper, set aside and keep warm.

Slice leeks into 1 ¼-in (3-cm) rounds, wash thoroughly. Melt butter in a large pan and sauté leeks 3 minutes over medium heat. Add a little chicken stock (or water) to help them to steam over medium heat until tender. Set aside and keep warm.

Cook pasta in a large pot of salted boiling water about 5 minutes. Place a spoonful of cauliflower purée in the centre of each plate, followed by leeks and topped with pasta. Melt some extra butter or warm truffle oil and drizzle over pasta and plate.

Serves 6.

Wild Boar Cassoulet, p. 95

Mains — Game and Meat

These tasty recipes for main-course dishes feature red meats and game. For a great taste of Italy, there is Il Piatto di Saltimbocca from La Perla in Dartmouth, a dish with three different meats. Or for the flavour of India, treat yourself to the delicious Noisette of Lamb from Onyx in Halifax or the Lamb Curry from the Pacific Rim Grille in Coquitlam. Try teaming the dishes in this chapter with a pasta or vegetable dish from one of the previous chapters, or with fresh seasonal vegetables of your choice.

When cooking meat and game, chefs tend to use prime cuts. These cuts of meat are the most tender and require only a short cooking time because they are very lean — they are best cooked medium rare. Lean meat is lower in fat and yields a more neutral taste, which allows the use of use a light touch with the flavouring. Use the ingredients lightly to enhance the natural flavour and produce a melodic mouth experience.

Alberta Beef Tenderloin
with Foie Gras Ravioli, Potato Soufflé, Porcini Jus

Teatro, Calgary, AB

This plate has a lot to say about Canada: Alberta beef, Quebec foie gras and PEI potatoes. All meld together to form a great taste.

Potato Soufflé
5 lb (2.5 kg) potatoes
2 oz (60 g) butter, soft
2 oz (60 g) flour
2 cups (500 mL) milk
4 egg whites
salt

Ravioli of Foie Gras
8 oz (240 g) fresh foie gras
¼ cup (60 mL) cream sherry
salt and white pepper
fresh pasta

Tenderloin and Porcini Jus
1 shallot, finely diced
1 tbsp (15 mL) butter
1 cup (250 mL) red wine
2 cups (500 mL) veal stock
1 tbsp (15 mL) red wine gastrique *
4 oz (120 g) dried porcinis

8 x 4 oz (120 g) beef tenderloin portions

Bake potatoes at 350ºF (180ºC). Coat inside of ramekins with a thin layer of butter. In a medium-sized pot make a roux with butter and flour, then add milk slowly to incorporate (beware of lumps). Bring to a slow boil. Pass cooked potatoes through a sieve to remove any lumps. Stir potatoes into milk mixture and cool slightly. Whisk egg whites until just starting to form peaks, then fold whites into potato mixture. Add salt to taste. Pour mix into ramekins and bake at 375ºF (190ºC) until it has risen slightly and the top is a golden brown.

Bring foie gras to room temperature, break apart gently and remove all veins. Marinate foie gras with sherry, salt and white pepper. Wrap in plastic and refrigerate overnight. Bring foie gras to room temperature again and roll tightly in plastic wrap, forming a log. Refrigerate until firm. Unwrap and slice log into 8 servings to form ravioli filling.

Roll pasta thinly and cut 16 equal-sized circles. Place a foie gras slice in the centre of each of 8 pasta rounds. Brush outside edge of pasta with water and place another pasta round on the top, sealing the edges with the end of a spoon. Cook in boiling salted water 3 minutes.

In a pan, sweat shallots with butter. Add red wine and reduce by half. Add veal stock and gastrique and bring to a boil. Turn down heat to a gentle simmer and add porcinis. Simmer and reduce until jus thickens.

Pan sear beef to desired doneness. Plate with potato soufflé beside tenderloin, lay ravioli gently on top, spoon porcini jus over top and accompany with fresh cooked vegetables tossed in butter.

* Gastrique is 1 oz (15 g) of sugar and 1 tbsp (15 mL) of red wine boiled and reduced together.

Serves 8.

Beef Tenderloin
with Shallot and Cabernet Sauce

Angeline's Inn and Spa, Bloomfield, ON

The rich taste of beef should be accompanied by a strong wine. The full body of cabernet is just right. Enjoy this course with a glass of the same cabernet used in the sauce for the full effect.

4 x 4 oz beef tenderloins
salt and pepper
1 tbsp (15 mL) canola oil
1 tbsp (15 mL) butter
2 tbsp (30 mL) diced shallots
¼ cup (60 mL) red wine
3 tbsp (45 mL) veal stock
2 tbsp (30 mL) butter
½ clove garlic, chopped
fresh cut chives

Season beef with salt and pepper. Heat oil in a skillet until very hot and sear beef on both sides, then finish in a 400°F (200°C) oven until desired doneness. Rest beef 5 minutes, keeping warm. Discard oil, add butter to skillet and sweat half the shallots until golden. Deglaze skillet with red wine, add veal stock and reduce until the liquid is the consistency of sauce. Add garlic and season with salt and pepper.

Serve tenderloins on plates, coated with finished sauce, and garnish with remaining chopped shallots and a sprinkling of fresh cut chives. Serve with any seasonal vegetable and potato.

Serves 4.

Elk
Medallions

Little Britt Inn, Britt, ON

The tenderloin of any animal is the most highly prized cut because of its tenderness. It is also always the leanest cut. In this dish the bacon adds flavour while helping the meat to remain moist. At the Little Britt Inn, the elk is served with mini rostis, the Swiss version of a potato pancake.

4 x 3 oz (120 g) elk tenderloins
8 slices bacon
2 oz (60 mL) olive oil
salt and pepper

Elderberry Jus
¼ cup (60 mL) beef stock
1 tbsp (15 mL) elderberry jelly

Mini Rostis
4 medium potatoes
salt
oil and butter for frying

Wrap elk in bacon, brush with olive oil and sprinkle with salt and pepper.

Sear meat in a very hot heavy-bottomed pan. Remove elk from the pan and set aside to keep warm.

Deglaze the cooking pan with beef stock, add jelly and reduce by one-half to make the jus.

Boil potatoes, about 10 minutes (until still hard in centre). Drain and cool completely.

Coarsely grate potatoes into a hot pan, forming a rosti 3- to 4-in (7.5- to 10-cm) in diameter. Fry both sides until golden brown on the outside and tender on the inside. Repeat to make 4 rostis.

Place a rosti on each plate, top with elk medallion and drizzle jus around the plate.

Serves 4.

Roasted Rabbit
Loin

Raincity Grill, Vancouver, BC

Pancetta is a type of cured Italian meat. It is that country's version of bacon without the smoked flavour. It adds a small amount of fat to keep the lean rabbit meat tender and moist. Quince is very bitter and requires cooking to enhance its natural taste.

Quince Stuffing
10 shallots
5 garlic cloves
4 tbsp (60 mL) butter
2 cups (500 mL) pine mushrooms
2 cups (500 mL) quince, peeled, cored and
    chopped
salt and pepper
2 tbsp (30 mL) fresh-picked thyme
½ cup (125 mL) brioche crumbs

Rabbit
6 slices pancetta
1 rabbit, deboned and butterflied
salt and pepper
3 tbsp (45 mL) vegetable oil

Rabbit Stock
bones from rabbit
1 small onion, peeled and chopped
1 carrot, peeled and chopped
1 rib of celery chopped

Rabbit and Pine Mushroom Reduction
15 shallots, sliced
2 tbsp (30 mL) vegetable oil
1 cup (250 mL) pine mushrooms
1 cup (250 mL) white wine
3 cups (750 mL) rabbit stock
1 sprig thyme
4 peppercorns
2 bay leaves

Yields 2 cups (500 mL)

½ lb (250 g) pine mushroom slices, to taste

To make the stuffing, sauté shallots and garlic in butter until soft in a medium-sized pan over medium-high heat. Add pine mushrooms and cook until tender, then add quince, cover and cook until quince is soft. Remove from heat and briefly blend mixture, being careful to keep texture coarse. Season with salt and pepper for taste and add thyme. Fold in brioche crumbs. Chill thoroughly before using.

Layer pancetta slices in two equal rows across a piece of plastic wrap. Place rabbit on pancetta and season with salt and pepper. Spoon a ½-in (1.5-cm) diameter strand of stuffing down the centre and use the plastic to help you roll rabbit up like a sushi roll. Tie the ends securely with twine and poach in a pot of boiling water 10 minutes. Cool, unwrap and sear in a hot pan in oil until golden on all sides. Roast in a 400ºF (200ºC) oven 8 minutes.

To make the stock, place all ingredients in a roasting pan, and cook in oven at 375ºF (190ºC) until bones are browned. Place in a large pot and cover with water. Simmer over medium heat 2 hours. Strain.

For the reduction, in a medium-sized pot sweat shallots in oil, add mushrooms and caramelize. Pour in wine and reduce by three-quarters. Add rabbit stock, thyme, peppercorns and bay leaves, reduce by half and strain.

Remove rabbit from the oven and let rest 5 minutes. Slice into 1 ½-in (4-cm) pieces and serve with seared pine mushroom slices and rabbit and pine mushroom reduction.

Serves 6.

Rack of Lamb
with Smoked Paprika, Potato and Yam Stack

Mahle House, Nanaimo, BC

The lamb and smoked bacon mustard sauce take subtle flavours to new heights. The slight bite of the Dijon mustard is wonderfully mellowed by the sweetness of the potato stack.

Double Smoked Bacon and Dijon Mustard Sauce

¼ lb (125 g) double smoked bacon
6 shallots, finely diced
8 cups (2 L) demi-glace
¼ cup (60 mL) heavy cream (35% m.f.)
3 tbsp (45 mL) Dijon mustard
salt and pepper

Mashed Potatoes

1 lb (500 g) potatoes
¼ cup (60 mL) light cream (18% m.f.)
6 cloves roasted garlic
¼ cup (60 mL) butter
sea salt and pepper to taste

2 lamb racks
2 tsp (10 mL) smoked paprika
sea salt
black pepper
3 tbsp (45 mL) olive oil
2 large yams

For the sauce, roughly chop bacon and sauté until half cooked. Add shallots and sauté until soft, then pour in demi-glace and reduce to half. Add cream and mustard and continue reducing to a saucelike consistency. Check seasoning and adjust to taste. Strain through a fine sieve and set aside.

Peel and cook potatoes in salted water until tender. When cooked, scald cream with garlic (heat cream and garlic and bring to a boil). Put potatoes through a ricer to make a very smooth mash, pour in garlic cream, add butter and stir until well combined. Season, set aside and keep warm until needed.

Season racks of lamb with smoked paprika, sea salt and black pepper. Sear in a little olive oil in sauté pan drain and bake in 500°F (260°C) oven, 15 minutes or until done to your preference. Remove racks from oven and let rest (covered with foil) 10 minutes.

Slice yams 1-in (2.5-cm) thick and steam until cooked, about 8 minutes, then sauté until lightly brown.

Form alternate layers of yam and mashed potato mixed with smoked paprika until stack is desired height.

Cut lamb racks into chops. Place a potato stack in centre of plate, circle with lamb chops and spoon bacon and mustard sauce around base of chops.

Serves 4.

Noisette of Lamb,
Moroccan Spice Rubbed, Slow Braised and Topped with Chimichurri

Onyx, Halifax, NS

Braising is the best way to add flavour to meats and make them fork tender. This recipe uses several fine, traditional spices to create a delicious marinade and sauce to perfectly complement the lamb.

Moroccan Lamb Spice
2 tbsp (30 mL) fennel seeds
2 tbsp (30 mL) cumin seeds, roasted
1 tbsp (15 mL) coriander seeds
½ tsp (2 mL) cinnamon stick, grated
2 cardamom pods, ground
½ tsp (2 mL) lemon salt
3 anise seed, ground
1 tsp (5 mL) turmeric
⅓ cup (85 mL) brown sugar
juice of ½ lime
½ (125 mL) cup olive oil

Braising
¼ cup (60 mL) olive oil
1 ¼ lb (600 g) noisette of lamb
3 cups (750 mL) dry red wine
2 cups (500 mL) chicken stock

Chimichurri
½ cup (125 mL) Italian parsley
1 ¼ tbsp (17 mL) olive oil
1 tsp (5 mL) lemon juice
1 clove garlic, minced
¼ shallot, medium, minced
1 ½ tsp (18 mL) sherry vinegar
¼ tsp (1 mL) red pepper flakes
salt
pepper, freshly ground

Yields 1 cup

Grind fennel, cumin and coriander seeds in a coffee grinder. Transfer to a large bowl and mix with remaining Moroccan lamb spice ingredients to form a marinade.

Marinate lamb in spices 6 hours. In a large roasting pan heat oil and sear lamb until browned all over. Pour in red wine and stock, cover with foil wrap and bake in a 300° F (150°C) oven until tender.

Combine all chimichurri ingredients in a food processor or blender and pulse into a smooth paste.

Slice lamb into 4 servings. Fan sliced lamb on each plate and spoon chimichurri sauce over the top.

Serves 4.

Lamb
Curry

Pacific Rim Grille, Coquitlam, BC

A trip to India comes to mind with this lamb dish. The lamb and curry combination is refreshed with cilantro at the end, making a hearty dish feel light.

1 x ½ lb (750 g) lamb shoulder, diced
salt and pepper
3 tbsp (45 mL) canola oil
1 small onion, diced
2 tbsp (30 mL) chopped garlic
2 tbsp (30 mL) chopped ginger
6 oz (180 g) canned crushed tomatoes
2 tbsp (30 mL) curry powder
2 tsp (10 mL) ground cumin seed
2 tsp (10 mL) ground coriander seed
1 large bunch fresh cilantro, chopped

Glazed Carrots
6 baby carrots, peeled
1 tbsp (15 mL) brown sugar
½ cup (125 mL) chicken stock
1 tbsp (15 mL) sliced chives
salt and pepper

Garlic Turnip Greens
4 tbsp (60 mL) olive oil
2 cloves garlic, sliced
2 lb (1 kg) turnip greens
salt
black pepper

Season lamb with salt and pepper. Heat canola oil in a large pan and brown lamb on all sides. Add all remaining ingredients except cilantro, bring to a simmer, cover and cook on low heat 45 minutes, or until lamb is cooked and tender. Stir in cilantro.

Prepare carrots by cooking in a covered frying pan over medium-high heat with brown sugar and chicken stock until carrots are tender. Uncover and cook until stock has reduced. Add chives and salt and pepper if needed.

In a large skillet heat olive oil over medium heat. Add garlic, turnip greens, salt and pepper to taste. Cook until just wilted.

Divide curried lamb between plates and serve carrots and turnip greens as side dishes.

Serves 4.

Il Piatto
di Saltimbocca

La Perla, Dartmouth, NS

Saltimbocca translates as "tastes so good it jumps into the mouth." A traditional dish from the Emilia Romana region of Italy, this plate features three different tastes.

6 slices prosciutto
12 fresh sage leaves
4 x 2 oz (60 g) veal scaloppini
4 x 2 oz (60 g) chicken scaloppini
4 x 2 oz (60 g) fillets of salmon
flour for dredging
olive oil for searing
1 cup (250 mL) dry white wine
1 cup (250 mL) demi-glace
salt and pepper
2 tbsp (30 mL) garlic butter
olive oil for frying

Cut prosciutto slices in half crosswise. Place a sage leaf on each piece of veal, chicken, and salmon and top with prosciutto. Lightly flour each and quickly sauté in oil both sides. Set aside and keep warm. Drain oil from the pan, add wine and reduce by half. Pour in demi-glace and reduce by half. Season with salt and pepper and whisk in garlic butter. Place one piece of veal, chicken, and salmon on each plate and spoon sauce over.

Serves 4.

Wild Boar
Cassoulet

Fleur de Sel, Lunenburg, NS

Cassoulet is a hearty stew, rich in pork and the all-important white beans. The lean wild boar and the pork fat are full of flavour and the beans are full of carbohydrates and proteins.

1 lb (500 g) parsnips
1 cup (250 mL) hot whipping cream
salt and pepper
4 cups (1 L) cooked white beans
1 cup (250 mL) whipping cream
4 wild boar chops, 1-in (2.5-cm) thick
1 cup (250 mL) diced pork fat
1 cup (250 mL) diced tomatoes
2 tbsp (30 mL) chopped parsley
2 cups (500 mL) beef stock
½ cup (125mL) whipping cream (second
   amount)
2 tbsp (30 mL) grainy mustard
fleur de sel
sprig of thyme

Peel and cook parsnips in salted water until soft. Place parsnips in a food processor and add hot cream. Blend and season with salt and pepper. Set purée aside.

Place half the beans and the first amount of cream in a pot, bring to a boil and purée with a hand blender. Set aside, keeping warm. In a large frying pan, sear chops 1 ½ minutes on each side, then place in a 350°F (180°C) oven, 4 minutes. Remove chops and tent with foil wrap to keep warm.

In the same pan, sauté pork fat until brown; add remaining beans, tomatoes and parsley. Add stock and reduce by half. Add second amount of cream and reduce again by half, whisking in mustard. Stir in bean purée.

Warm parsnip purée and spoon a portion onto centre of the plate. Place cassoulet on top of purée. Surround with mustard sauce. Place chop on top and garnish with fleur de sel and thyme.

Serves 4.

Veal Cheeks
with Braised Red Cabbage

Grosvenor's, Southampton, ON

A somewhat German influenced dish. The red cabbage adds a great accent to the richness of the veal cheeks.

2 lb (1 kg) veal cheeks
2 cups (500 mL) red wine
4 cups (1 L) beef stock
salt and pepper
1 small onion, diced
1 medium carrot, diced
½ small celery root, diced
1 bulb garlic, cut in half
1 tbsp (15 mL) black peppercorns
1 tsp (5 mL) fennel seed
1 tbsp (15 mL) mustard seed
4 rosemary stems

Braised Red Cabbage
1 red cabbage, shredded
1 red onion, sliced
¼ cup (60 mL) brown sugar
small piece bacon rind
¼ cup (60 mL) red wine vinegar
½ cup (125 mL) red wine

Vegetables
6 blue potatoes
¼ cup (65 mL) olive oil
salt and pepper

30 haricots vert
1 lb (500 g) chanterelles
3 oz (120 g) butter

Remove silver skin from veal cheeks. In a large pot mix wine and stock together and marinate cheeks overnight. Remove cheeks and dry well. Generously season with salt and pepper and sear in a hot pan until nicely browned. Place back in marinade. Sauté onion, carrot, celery root, garlic, peppercorns, fennel and mustard seeds and add to marinade with rosemary. Let cheeks cook very slowly over low heat or in the oven at 275°F (135°C), 5 to 6 hours. Cool cheeks in liquid.

In a large pan sweat cabbage and red onion. Add brown sugar, bacon rind, vinegar and red wine and cook slowly until soft. Remove bacon rind and discard. Season to taste.

Boil potatoes until half cooked and roast with olive oil, salt and pepper until tender. Blanch haricots vert. Sauté chanterelles in butter until soft.

Divide mushrooms, beans, cabbage and potatoes on the plates. Remove cheeks from marinade and slice ½-in (1-cm) thick. Add slices of cheeks and spoon sauce (the marinade) over.

Serves 6.

Venison Loin with Juniper,
Celeriac and Mascarpone Cheese Purée,
Roasted Winter Fruits with Maple Syrup and Thyme

Signatures, Ottawa, ON

The winter fruits that accompany the venison help to bring out similar flavours in the meat. Combined with the earthiness of the celeriac and the sweet richness of mascarpone, the layers of flavours on the plate meld in perfect harmony.

Venison

1 lb (500 g) venison loin
salt and pepper
1 tbsp (15 mL) ground juniper
oil for searing

Winter Fruits

1 quince
1 pear
1 apple
2 tbsp (30 mL) butter
1 sprig of thyme, chopped
4 tbsp (60 mL) maple syrup

Celeriac Purée

¼ celeriac, peeled
salt and pepper
3 oz (90 g) mascarpone

Sauce

1 small onion
1 tbsp (15 ml) olive oil
10 juniper berries
1 tbsp (15 mL) peppercorns
1 tbsp (15 mL) red currant jelly
1 ¼ cups (300 mL) red wine
1 bay leaf
1 ¼ cups (300 mL) beef stock
2 oz (60 g) butter
salt and pepper

Cut venison into 3 oz (100 g) portions, season with salt and pepper, then coat with ground juniper. Sear in a sauté pan and cook to desired doneness. Set aside to rest.

Peel quince, pear and apple, cut into quarters and remove cores. Cook quince in slightly sweetened water until *al dente*. Melt butter in a sauté pan and cook pear and apple until coloured. Add thyme, quince and maple syrup and finish cooking in a 400°F (200°C) oven 2 to 3 minutes.

Dice and cook celeriac in boiling salted water until tender. Strain and place in the bowl of a food processor and mix with mascarpone cheese until smooth. Adjust seasoning to taste.

For the sauce, cut onion into small dice and sweat in a medium sauce pot with 1 tbsp olive oil, juniper berries and peppercorns until lightly coloured. Add jelly, red wine and bay leaf and reduce by half. Add stock and reduce until syrupy. Strain through a fine sieve and whisk in butter. Adjust seasoning if needed. Keep warm.

Slice each venison portion into three medallions and arrange on one side of the plate. Make a quenelle of celeriac purée and place in the centre. Arrange winter fruit above purée. Finish by spooning sauce around meat.

Serves 5.

Roast Loin of Venison
with Mocha Infused Blueberry Demi

Tempest, Wolfville, NS

Coffee has long been used in the cooking of meats. It adds a certain richness to the flavour, and if the meat has a little too much "wild," it will help mellow the flavour.

1 x 4 lb (1.8kg) venison saddle
1 tbsp (30 mL) olive oil
1 tsp (5 mL) butter
salt and pepper

Marinade
1 cup (250 mL) red wine
1 onion, chopped
1 tsp (5 mL) juniper berries, crushed
1 tsp (5 mL) black peppercorns
¼ cup (60 mL) soy sauce (optional)
½ bunch fresh thyme
2 tbsp (30 mL) olive oil

Mocha Infused Blueberry Sauce
2 large onions, chopped
2 large carrots, chopped
4 ribs celery, chopped
bones from venison
2 tbsp (30 mL) tomato paste
4 bay leaves
½ bunch fresh thyme
1 cup (250 mL) red wine
4 cups (1 L) water

½ cup (125 mL) blueberries, frozen
1 tsp (5 mL) instant coffee crystals
3 tbsp (45 mL) butter
2 tbsp (30 mL) blueberry jam (optional)
salt
Tabasco sauce

Yields 2 cups (500 mL)

Three days before serving, de-bone saddle of venison. In a zip-lock bag large enough to hold venison, combine all marinade ingredients. Marinate venison in refrigerator until the day you are planning to serve it. On that day, remove from marinade and pat dry.

In a large frying pan on medium-high heat, add olive oil and butter. Season dried loin with salt and pepper. When butter starts to brown add loin to pan and sear on all sides until brown, about 5 minutes. Remove to a roasting pan and roast in a 425°F (215°C) degree oven, 5 minutes for rare to medium-rare. Remove venison from oven and let rest 10 minutes in a warm place. Add any accumulated pan juice to sauce.

For the sauce, first make a stock. In a large roasting pan, mix onions, carrots and celery and lay venison bones on top. Roast bones in a moderately hot oven, 425°F (215°C), until brown, about 15 minutes. Cover bones with tomato paste using a pastry brush, and roast another 5 to 10 minutes. Remove all ingredients into a large stockpot. Add herbs. Deglaze roasting pan with red wine and add to stockpot. Cover bones and vegetables with water and bring to a boil. Reduce heat and simmer 4 hours.

Strain stock into a tall container and chill. When completely cold, remove any coagulated fat from surface of stock and discard. Return stock to a pot on the stove. Bring to a boil and reduce to 1 ½ cups. Add blueberries and coffee and whisk in butter. Add jam and whisk in (optional). Season with salt and Tabasco sauce.

Slice and serve venison topped with sauce.

Serves 6.

Molten Chocolate, p. 123

Desserts

Dessert — generally everyone's favourite part of dinner! This is the course that can either make or break a dinner party. Flavours here can be delightfully intense, like the Chocolate Crème Brûlée from Casa Bella in Gananoque, or comforting and homey like the Blueberry Bread Pudding from Chives in Halifax. The refreshing Lemon Tart with Fresh Raspberries from Angeline's Inn and Spa in Bloomfield is very pleasing after a multi-course dinner. Or as a fun end to a fabulous evening, try a taste of Newfoundland with Aqua's Screech Pie with Molasses Chantilly.

Lemon Tart
with Fresh Raspberries

Angeline's Inn and Spa, Bloomfield, ON

The tartness of the lemons and raspberries are a great way to end a rich dinner. Look for a limoncello or lemon grappa to accompany this dessert.

1 frozen pie shell
juice of ½ orange
juice of 1 lemon
1 tsp (5 mL) orange zest
zest of 1 lemon
2 egg yolks
¾ cup (200 mL) heavy cream (35% m.f.)
3 oz (90 g) sugar
3 tbsp (45 mL) crystal sugar
1 tbsp (15 mL) butter
fresh seasonal raspberries (enough for 8 people)

Pre-bake pie shell half way.

In a glass bowl whisk orange juice, lemon juice, orange and lemon zests and egg yolks to combine.

In a nonreactive pot, bring cream and sugar to a boil. Slowly add hot cream into yolk mixture while whisking to avoid curdling, then transfer mixture back to the cooking pot. Stir gently and constantly with a rubber spatula over low heat until mixture starts to thicken slightly, taking care not to curdle yolks. Whisk in butter.

Pour mixture into pie shell, bake in a 275°F (135°C) oven 8 to 10 minutes or until filling is firm. Remove pie, place on cooling rack, sprinkle with crystal sugar and brûlée with blowtorch. Refrigerate 2 to 3 hours and serve with fresh raspberries.

Serves 6 to 8.

Pineapple
Crumble

Aerie Resort, Malahat, BC

Sweet and tart pineapple gets new life when poached in syrup, and the rich goat cheese adds a mellow element. Choose a cheese that is young and creamy.

Poached Pineapple

4 cups (1 L) sugar
4 cups (1 L) water
1 lemon peel
1 vanilla bean
zest of 1 lime
1 stalk lemongrass
1 pineapple, peeled and cored

Goat Cheese Filling

1 cup (250 mL) goat cheese
1 egg
¼ cup (60 mL) sugar
2 tsp (10 mL) vanilla
¼ cup (60 mL) heavy cream (35% m.f.)

Crumble Topping

2 cups (500 mL) oats
1 cup (250 mL) brown sugar
1 tsp (5 mL) vanilla
¼ cup (60 mL) flour
1 cup (250 mL) melted butter

Place sugar, water, lemon peel and vanilla in a large pot and bring to a boil. Add lime zest and lemongrass and let flavours infuse. Slice four pineapple rings, 1 ½-in (4-cm) thick. Place pineapple rings in poaching liquid. Reduce heat to medium and simmer for 8 to 10 minutes until syrup thickens. Cool and reserve.

In the bowl of a mixer mix all goat cheese filling ingredients until just combined. Set aside.

Mix all crumble topping ingredients in a bowl and set aside.

Lay some parchment paper on a small baking tray. Build the crumble on the tray using a round mould slightly larger than the pineapple rings. Place a pineapple ring in the mould and fill the centre of the ring with some of the goat cheese filling. Make sure that the rings are flat and that the filling stays in the centre. Add and pack the crumble mixture to the top and remove the mould. Repeat with remaining pineapple rings. Bake in a 350°F (180°C) oven for 8 to 10 minutes, or until topping turns golden brown. Remove the mould and dress each dessert with poaching syrup.

Serves 4.

Apple
Strudel

Pacific Rim Grille, Coquitlam, BC

Tart Granny Smith apples and cranberries are
tamed by the earthy walnuts, star anise and the
butteriness of the puff pastry in this strudel.

2 lb (1 kg) granny smith apples
1 cup (250 mL) dry white wine
½ cup (125 mL) apple juice
¼ cup (60 mL) sugar
2 tbsp (30 mL) ground cinnamon
2 star anise
1 cup (250 mL) raisins
¼ cup (60 mL) lemon juice
½ cup (125 mL) dried cranberries
½ cup (125 mL) walnuts
1 lb (500 g) prepared puff pastry
1 lightly beaten egg (egg wash)
½ cup (125 mL) brown sugar

Peel, core and dice apples. In a large pan, place
apples, wine, apple juice, sugar, spices, raisins,
lemon juice and cranberries. Cook until apples
are soft, and all liquid has evaporated. Add
walnuts and cool. Roll out pastry in a rectangle,
⅛-in (3-mm) thick. With the long side in front of
you, spoon cooled apple mix down the pastry,
evenly and along the front edge. Roll pastry into
a log. Brush with egg wash and sprinkle with
brown sugar. Bake in a 350°F (180°C) oven until
golden brown.

Serves 6.

Blueberry
Bread Pudding

Chives Canadian Bistro, Halifax, NS

A warm country feel is what you get from bread pudding, and the little bursts of blueberry sauce are very homey.

3 large eggs
1 ½ cup (375 mL) light cream (10% m.f.)
1 tsp (5 mL) allspice
1 tbsp (15 mL) vanilla
½ cup (125 mL) brown sugar
1 cup (250 mL) blueberries
4 cups (1 L) cubed dried bread

Blueberry Sauce
2 cups (500 mL) blueberries
½ cup (125 mL) sugar
2 oz (60 mL) brandy

In a large bowl whisk eggs, cream, allspice, vanilla and sugar together. Mix in blueberries and soak bread in the mix 1 hour. Spray a loaf pan with nonstick spray and pour in bread/egg mixture. Place the loaf pan in a larger pan containing 1 in (2.5 cm) of water. Bake in a 300°F (150°C) oven 30 minutes.

In a large pot cook berries with sugar until they release their juice and become a sauce. Remove from heat and add brandy. Serve alongside bread pudding.

Serves 4.

Cranberry
Cake

Little Britt Inn, Britt, ON

Individual desserts are making a huge impact on the dining scene. Not only do they look great, they are also easily plated — there's no fuss cutting into portions. And they can be warmed very quickly with a few minutes in the oven while the coffee is brewing.

3 cups (750 mL) all-purpose flour
4 tsp (20 mL) baking powder
½ tsp (3 mL) salt
1 ½ cup (375 mL) sugar
3 cups (750 mL) fresh cranberries
1 ½ cup (375 mL) whole milk (3.25% m.f.)
1 ½ tsp (8 mL) vanilla
butter for greasing pans

Butter Sauce
¾ cup (190 mL) butter
1 ½ cup (375 mL) sugar
¾ cup (190 mL) milk
3 tbsp (45 mL) Cointreau

Yields 2 cups(500 mL)

Cranberry Relish
2 cups (500 mL) whole cranberries
zest of 2 oranges
juice of 2 oranges
¼ cup (60 mL) sugar

Yields 2 cups (500 mL)

Preheat oven to 375°F (190°C). Grease and flour muffin pans. In a large bowl combine all dry ingredients together with cranberries. Pour in milk and vanilla, stir until just combined and fill the muffin pans. Bake 35 to 40 minutes, or until a tester comes out clean.

In a medium-sized pot, combine all butter sauce ingredients and bring to a boil over high heat, stirring constantly. Remove from heat and keep warm.

Mix all cranberry relish ingredients in a glass bowl and allow to macerate 24 hours, covered and refrigerated.

When all the components are ready, pour warm butter sauce over cakes and spoon relish around them.

Serves 8.

Gingerbread Cake
with Green Tea Ice Cream

Tempest, Wolfville, NS

Some say gingerbread is best in the fall and winter. I say it is great all year round. The soft gentle balance of the gingerbread and the green tea ice cream make for a treat anytime.

1 ¼ cup (310 mL) all-purpose flour
2 ½ tsp (12 mL) ground ginger
1 ½ tsp (7 mL) ground cinnamon
1 tsp (5 mL) baking soda
¼ tsp (1 mL) ground cloves
¼ tsp (1 mL) salt
¼ cup (60 mL) chopped crystallized ginger
½ cup (125 ml) vegetable oil
½ cup (125 mL) molasses
½ cup (125 mL) dark brown sugar
1 large egg
1 ½ tsp (7 mL) grated lemon peel
½ cup (125 mL) boiling water
powdered sugar
butter, for greasing baking pan

Green Tea Ice Cream
2 cups (500 mL) heavy cream (35% m.f.)
1 cup (250 mL) whole milk (3.25% m.f.)
¼ tsp (1 mL) salt
6 large eggs
⅔ cup (190 mL) sugar
2 tbsp (30 mL) powdered green tea

Yields 4 cups (1 L)

Preheat oven to 350°F (180°C). Butter and flour an 8-in-square (20-cm) metal baking pan. Whisk flour, ginger, cinnamon, baking soda, cloves and salt in a medium bowl to blend well, then whisk in crystallized ginger. Whisk oil, molasses and brown sugar in a separate large bowl to blend, then whisk in egg and lemon peel. Gradually whisk in flour mix, then boiling water. Transfer batter to the prepared pan.

Bake until a tester inserted into centre of cake comes out clean, about 30 minutes. Cool cake 15 minutes. Cut into squares and sift powdered sugar over. (Cake can be made one day ahead. Cool completely, cover and store at room temperature.)

Bring cream, milk and salt to a boil in a heavy 3- to 4-quart (3- to 4- litre) saucepan and remove from heat. Whisk together eggs, sugar and tea in a bowl (tea will not dissolve completely), then add 1 cup (250 mL) of hot cream mixture in a slow stream, whisking vigorously. Whisk custard into remaining cream mixture in saucepan. Cook over moderately low heat, stirring constantly with a wooden spoon until thick enough to coat the back of a spoon, and registering 170°F (80°C) on an instant-read thermometer. Do not boil.

Immediately pour custard through a fine sieve into a metal bowl, then cool to room temperature, stirring occasionally. Chill, covered, at least 1 hour. Freeze in ice cream maker, then transfer to an airtight container and place in freezer to harden.

Serve cake warm or at room temperature with green tea ice cream topping.

Serves 4.

Crema Catalana Foam
with Blood Oranges and Shaved Chocolate

Black Cat Café, Ottawa, ON

This dessert is a new way of making a quick and easy mousse. The yellow saffron goes well with the purple red blood orange, and the orange chocolate flavour is classic.

8 egg yolks
5 tbsp (75 mL) honey
1 cup (250 mL) heavy cream (35% m.f.)
1 vanilla bean, scraped
1 tsp (5 mL) saffron
1 cup (250 mL) milk (3.25% m.f.)
¼ tsp (1 mL) salt
4 blood oranges, segmented
2 oz (60 g) Valrhona dark chocolate (70% cocoa
    solids)
sprig of lovage

In a bowl, whisk eggs with honey until smooth and pale. In a saucepan bring cream, scraped vanilla bean, saffron, milk and salt to a simmer. Remove from heat and let cream infuse with the flavours 5 minutes. Bring to a simmer again, and slowly add hot cream to egg mixture while whisking to avoid curdling. Cook over very low heat until thickened. Strain through a fine sieve and chill in an ice bath until very cold.

Transfer cream to a whipping cream canister, fill to halfway mark and load with 1 gas charger. Refrigerate 1 hour before using.

Place blood orange segments on serving plates and pipe Catalan foam* on top. Shave a little dark chocolate on top and serve with a sprig of lovage.

*Catalan foam will keep up to 2 days refrigerated.

Serves 4.

Crème Brûlée
with Rum and Cola Reduction

Onyx, Halifax, NS

Chefs today are always coming up with new ways to serve old favourites, like this spin on crème brûlée. When reduced the cola produces a sweet syrup and the rum adds a bite.

3 cups (750 mL) heavy cream (35% m.f.)
3 oz (90 g) sugar
¼ vanilla pod
pinch salt
6 egg yolks

Rum and Cola Reduction
1 can cola
2 oz (60 mL) dark rum

Heat cream, sugar, vanilla and salt in a medium-sized pot at medium-high heat. Place egg yolks in a large bowl and slowly pour in warm cream mixture. Stir to make a custard. Pour custard into ramekins. Bake in a water bath, 15 minutes covered, then 20 minutes uncovered or until set. Remove and cool. Refrigerate at least 4 hours.

In a large frying pan reduce cola and rum to a syrupy consistency. Cool and pour over custards.

Serves 4.

Screech
Pie

Aqua, St John's, NL

There is a tradition in Newfoundland of being "screeched in." It involves drinking the famous screech rum and kissing a codfish. Lots of fun and a great party – but if you prefer something a little sweeter, you could just enjoy the taste of screech from this pie.

Crust
¼ cup (60 mL) unsalted butter (melted)
1 cup (250 mL) gingersnap cookies (processed)

Filling
2 tbsp (30 mL) gelatin
3 tbsp (45 mL) water
14 oz (450 mL) evaporated milk
¼ cup (60 mL) whole milk (3.25% m.f.)
¾ cup (190 mL) sugar
½ cup (125 mL) whole milk (3.25%) (second amount)
2 egg yolks
3 oz (90 g) semi-sweet chocolate
¼ cup (60 mL) Newfoundland screech
1 vanilla bean, scraped

Crystallized Ginger and Rhubarb Jam
1 cup (250 mL) rhubarb
1 tbsp (15 mL) finely chopped crystallized ginger
1 tsp (10 mL) lemon juice
2 tbsp (30 mL) honey
1 star anise

Molasses Chantilly
1 cup (250 mL) heavy cream (35% m.f.)
½ vanilla bean
2 tbsp (30 mL) icing sugar
¼ cup (60 mL) molasses

Heat oven to 350°F (180°C). In a bowl mix melted butter and gingersnaps together. Press into the bottom of 6 2-inch (5-cm) ring moulds to about one-quarter of their depth. Bake for 10 minutes on a cookie tray. Cool.

Pour evaporated milk into a shallow dish and place in freezer until it becomes slightly mushy at the sides. Soften gelatin in ¼ cup (60 mL) milk. Combine sugar, ½ cup (125 mL) milk, egg yolks, and softened gelatin on top of a double boiler and mix well. Cook over the simmering water until gelatin dissolves and mixture thickens slightly. Remove from heat. In a separate pan melt chocolate and add to gelatin mixture. Allow mixture to chill until it thickens slightly. Whip chilled evaporated milk until thick and fold whipped evaporated milk, rum and vanilla seeds into chocolate mixture. Pour on top of gingersnap crust, about three-quarters of the mould depth, and chill thoroughly.

Combine all rhubarb jam ingredients in a saucepan and simmer until slightly thick and syrupy, about 10 to 15 minutes. Chill.

Place all chantilly ingredients in the bowl of a mixer with a whip attachment. Whip until mixture forms stiff peaks.

To present pie, remove from mould in the centre of a plate, spoon jam around pie and add a serving of molasses chantilly on top.

Serves 6.

Panna
Cotta

La Perla, Dartmouth, NS

Panna cotta is Italian-style cooked cream. This recipe is one I made while working at Hotel Marchi in Modena. It is a version of custard but set with gelatin instead of egg yolks.

1 package gelatin ¼ cup (60 mL) whole milk
  (3.25%)
3 cups (750 mL) heavy cream (35%)
½ cup (125 mL) sugar
piece of vanilla bean
pan release spray

Spray 4 ramekins with pan release and set aside. Bloom gelatin in milk and set aside. In a heavy-bottomed pot, bring cream, sugar and vanilla bean to a boil. Add bloomed gelatin to cream, stirring to break down gelatin. Pour into ramekins and refrigerate until set, about 2 hours.

Serve with caramel sauce or fruit purée.

Serves 4.

Torte di Cioccolata con Pera
(Warm Chocolate Torte With Pear)

Charlotte Lane Café, Shelburne, NS

A true sign of a chef's European background is the combination of chocolate and pear. Not often seen or heard of in North America, it's a genuine treat as the flavours just meld together.

3 pears
2 cups (500mL) simple syrup*
2 lb (1 kg) dark chocolate
1 lb (500 g) butter
10 large eggs
6 oz (180 g) sugar
1 tbsp (15 mL) cinnamon
1 tsp (5 mL) ground ginger
2 tsp (10 mL) vanilla
zest of 2 oranges

Preheat oven to 375°F (190°C), and grease a 10-inch (25-cm) spring form pan. Peel, core and dice pears. Cook in syrup until soft, remove from liquid and cool.

In a double boiler, melt chocolate and butter and set aside. In the bowl of an upright mixer whip eggs, sugar, cinnamon, ginger, vanilla and zest until tripled in volume. Fold batter into chocolate and pour into the prepared pan until half full. Add a layer of cooked pears and pour remaining batter over, filling pan three-quarters full. Bake 30 to 35 minutes, remove from oven and cool.

* Simple syrup is equal amounts of water and sugar brought to a boil.

Serves 6.

Profiteroles with Pistachio and Lime Gelato
and a Caraibe Valrhona Chocolate Puddle

Brookstreet, Ottawa, ON

Profiteroles are little shells that hold some sort of filling. Here the gelato is rich and creamy, with a hint of lime to spark the senses. Combined with semi-sweet chocolate sauce, it makes the perfect ending to any dinner.

Profiterole shells

1 cup (250 mL) water
¼ cup (60 g) sweet butter
¼ tsp (1 mL) salt
1 cup (250 mL) all-purpose flour
4 large eggs
1 lightly beaten egg (egg wash)

Chocolate Puddle

6 ½ oz (200 g) Valrhona chocolate
1 cup (250 mL) heavy cream (35% m.f.)

Pistachio and Lime Gelato

4 cups (1L) milk
½ cup (125 mL) sugar
¼ cup (60 mL) lime juice
10 oz (300 g) pistachios, ground

Plate Assembly

icing sugar for dusting
berries for garnish (whatever is fresh)

In a medium saucepan, combine water, butter and salt and bring to a boil. Add flour and stir with a wooden spoon until thoroughly combined. Continue to stir over medium heat, about 3 minutes.

Transfer dough to an upright mixer with a paddle. Mix 2 minutes on low setting. Add eggs one at a time until fully combined, about 4 to 6 minutes.

Using a small spoon form small puffs about ¾ in (2 cm) in diameter on a parchment-lined baking sheet. Brush each ball with egg wash. Bake in a 350°F (180°C) convection oven 30 minutes, or until golden brown. Cool and reserve. Using a knife slice profiteroles in half crosswise.

Chop chocolate coarsely. In the top of a double boiler over simmering water, place cream and chocolate and stir until melted. Keep warm.

For the ice cream, bring 3 cups of milk to a boil in a medium, heavy-bottomed saucepan over medium heat. In a bowl place remaining cup of milk, sugar and lime juice and stir until combined. Pour hot milk into the bowl, stir and return to saucepan. Stir constantly and cook 3

minutes. Place nuts in a large bowl and pour hot milk mixture over. Cool, cover and refrigerate. When cold place in an ice cream maker and churn.

Fill each profiterole with ice cream and place four pieces on a shallow plate. Drizzle warmed chocolate sauce over profiteroles. Dust with icing sugar and some berries. Serve immediately.

Serves 4 to 6.

Triple Chocolate
Cake

Grosvenor's, Southampton, ON

This cake gives three very distinct sensations. The chocolate base is a little crisp, followed by a coffee-tasting layer and finally the sensation of chocolate and cream.

Chocolate Shortbread Base

1 ½ cups (375 mL) unsalted butter
1 cup (250 mL) sugar
2 ½ cups (625 mL) all-purpose flour
4 ½ tbsp cocoa powder
¾ tsp (4 mL) cinnamon
½ tsp (2 mL) salt
¼ tsp (1 mL) baking soda

Coffee Layer

19 oz (580 g) dark chocolate
½ cup (125 mL) espresso
¾ cup (190 mL) sugar
6 large eggs
1 cup (250 mL) heavy cream (35% m.f.)

Ganache Layer

2 cups (500 mL) heavy cream (35% m.f.)
1 lb (500 g) dark chocolate, chopped

Preheat oven to 300°F (150°C) and place a pan of water on bottom rack. Line a 13-in x 10-in pan (33-cm x 25-cm) with parchment paper or foil wrap, allowing 2 in (5 cm) to overhang. In a large bowl cream butter and sugar together, add all remaining ingredients and mix, press in the bottom of prepared pan, and chill 30 minutes.

In the top of a double boiler melt chocolate and espresso together over hot (not boiling) water and set aside. In a large bowl combine sugar and eggs; stir over hot water (warmed eggs are easier to whisk), remove and whisk until light and fluffy, then fold into melted chocolate. Whip cream to stiff peaks and fold into chocolate mixture. Pour over shortbread crust and bake, covered with foil, 45 minutes. Remove from oven and cool. Refrigerate until completely cold.

For the ganache, heat cream over medium-high heat. Remove from heat, add chocolate and let it melt, stirring with a wire whisk until smooth.

Pour ganache over cooled cake and allow to set 2 hours. Remove from the pan and cut into six sections. Serve with strawberry coulis and vanilla gelato.

Serves 6.

Molten Chocolate
with Chocolate Gelato and Fresh Berries

Il Mulino, Toronto, ON

Warm chocolate flowing like lava and cool
decadent chocolate gelato will get all the
compliments any dinner host wants.

1 lb (500 g) dark chocolate (70% cocoa solids)
5 tbsp (75 g) sweet butter
7 whole eggs
7 egg yolks
5 tbsp (75 g) all-purpose flour
2 cups (500 mL) rich chocolate gelato
seasonal berries

Combine chocolate and butter and melt in a
double boiler. In a bowl, lightly whisk eggs and
yolks and add slowly to chocolate and butter,
then whisk in flour. Pour chocolate into moulds
and bake 5 to 7 minutes in a 500°F (290°C)
oven. The centre should be molten.

Garnish with a scoop of chocolate gelato and
fresh berries.

Serves 4

Red Wine and Chocolate Fondant
with Mascarpone Gelato

Fleur De Sel, Lunenburg, NS

To end an exquisite dinner, chocolate does the trick. Add a syrup of red wine and a gelato of mascarpone and things just get better. A glass of tawny port completes the encounter.

Fondant
4 x ½ oz (140 g) semi-sweet chocolate
2 oz (60 g) butter
2 eggs
2 egg yolks
5 tbsp (75 mL) sugar
1 tbsp (15 mL) flour

Red Wine Syrup
1 cup (250 mL) red wine
½ cup (125 mL) sugar

Mascarpone Gelato
1 ¼ cup (300 mL) milk
5 tbsp (75 mL) mascarpone
5 tbsp (75 mL) cream cheese

In the top of a double boiler melt chocolate and butter. In a small bowl whisk eggs, yolks and sugar, then add to chocolate and butter mixture. Whisk to combine, stir in flour and cool at room temperature. Generously butter four 6-oz (180-g) ramekins and divide batter among them. Bake at 400°F (200°C) 7 to 9 minutes, until top feels like a poached egg.

In a small pot, bring wine and sugar to a boil. Reduce by one-half and cool.

Place all gelato ingredients in the bowl of a food processor and blend until smooth. Pour mixture into an ice cream maker and churn until just set. Place in freezer until needed.

Turn each fondant onto a plate, garnish with red wine syrup and a scoop of mascarpone gelato and serve immediately.

Serves 4.

Chocolate Crème
Brûlée

Casa Bella, Gananoque, ON

Crème brûlée is one of those desserts that will
be around forever. The addition of chocolate
just makes a great dessert even better.

4 cups (1 L) heavy cream (35% m.f.)
12 oz (340 g) dark chocolate
10 egg yolks
¾ cup (190 mL) white sugar

Preheat oven to 325°F (170°C). In a saucepan
heat cream. In a double boiler, melt chocolate.
Whisk cream and chocolate together until
smooth. Whisk hot mixture into egg yolks a little
at a time to prevent eggs from curdling. Strain
custard mixture through a medium-fine sieve.

Divide custard mixture between 10 ramekins and
place in a *bain-marie* with a 1-in (2.5-cm) layer of
hot water. Cover loosely with aluminium foil and
bake 20 to 30 minutes, or until just set. Cool.

Just before serving, sprinkle a thin layer of white
sugar over surface of crème brûlée. Using a
blowtorch caramelize the sugar to form a
golden to dark-brown crust, which will harden
as it cools. Serve immediately.

Serves 10.

Index

Photo Credits

Photos by Alanna Jankov, with the exception of the following:
Kelly Cline: 51; Meghan Collins: 2, 4, 7, 31, 41, 45, 71, 84, 101, 117, 119; Tammy Fancy: 1, 8, 10, 13, 14, 22, 27, 35, 36-7, 39, 53, 57, 63, 64, 69, 75; Ekaterina Fribus: 115; iStock Photography: 23